Knits

to *Give*

Knits to Give

30 Knitted Gifts Made with Love

Debbie Bliss

Photography by Penny Wincer

TRAFALGAR SQUARE
North Pomfret, Vermont

Contents

After working for many years as a hand-knit designer, I sometimes struggle to recapture the sheer joy of knitting that comes from creating a project with only self-imposed deadlines as opposed to commercial ones. However, every time I pick up my knitting needles to make something for a family member or friend, I instantly feel that connection with the recipient: what it is that makes them dear to me. This is combined with the hope and anticipation that they will be delighted with my homemade gift, as it has been considered with care and my time and effort has been pored into producing something unique, created just for them.

Each week I hold a very informal knitting group, where I meet up with friends at a local bar-restaurant. These weekly craft meetings came about because I was meeting so many young mothers, all of whom wanted to take up knitting in order to make things for their new babies. Each one of them was a complete novice knitter. Mia, the amazing stylist for this book, started off by making simple squares so she could practice different stitch patterns. Once she had perfected a variety of stitches, Mia sewed all the squares together to make a patchwork blanket. She gave this finished knitted blanket to a mother-to-be friend at her baby shower. Her friend's overwhelming response to this one-off, hand-crafted present taught Mia—until now renowned for her skills as a shopper rather than as a maker—the joy of both making and giving. It also reminded me once again just how pleasureable gift-giving can be.

The projects in Knits to Give have been divided into chapters—For Her, For Him, For Baby, For Kids, For the Home—and are a mix of accessories, simple garments, toys, and homewares. A broad range that will hopefully provide a gift solution for even the most difficult to buy for. Many of the knits are simple and quick to make, because there are always those birthdays or special anniversaries that we are only reminded of shortly before they occur. Other projects are more time-consuming to make, but that will be cherished forever.

In an age of the "life on the go," bouncing between family, friends, and work commitments, the easy option is often to grab a little something and wrap it quickly before heading off to a get-together. But set aside some time, choose an appropriate pattern, pick a favorite color yarn, and discover how rewarding making something special for someone special in your life can be.

Debbie Bliss

Types of Yarn

The yarns I have chosen for the designs in this book range from my organic cotton to cashmerinos and pure wools, each with their own contribution to make to the designs. It may be that they give crisp stitch detail in a simple pattern, such as the seed stitch table mats worked in cotton, or provide softness and coziness in a baby shawl.

Unless you are using up your stash to make the smaller items in this book, make the effort to buy the yarn stated in the pattern. Each of these designs has been created with a specific yarn in mind.

A different yarn may not produce the same quality of fabric or have the same wash and wear properties. From an aesthetic point of view, the clarity of a subtle stitch pattern may be lost if a pattern is knitted in an inferior yarn. However, there may be occasions when a knitter needs to substitute a yarn—if there is an allergy to wool, for example—and so the following is a guideline to making the most informed choices.

Always buy a yarn that is the same weight as that given in the pattern: replace a double knitting with a double knitting, for example, and check that the gauge of both yarns is the same.

Where you are substituting a different fiber, be aware of the design. A cable pattern knitted in cotton when worked in wool will pull in because of the greater elasticity of the yarn and so the fabric will become narrower; this will alter the proportions of the garment.

Check the yardage of the yarn. Yarns that weigh the same may have different lengths in the ball, so you may need to buy more or less yarn.

Descriptions of my yarns used in this book and a guide to their weights and types are given on page 12.

Debbie Bliss Angel:
* A lightweight mohair-blend yarn.
* 76% superkid mohair, 24% silk.
* Approximately 218yd (200m)/⅞oz (25g) ball.

Debbie Bliss Baby Cashmerino:
* A fine-weight yarn.
* 55% merino wool, 33% microfiber, 12% cashmere.
* Approximately 137yd (125m)/1¾oz (50g) ball.

Debbie Bliss Bella:
* A double-knitting-weight yarn.
* 85% cotton, 10% silk, 5% cashmere.
* Approximately 104yd (95m)/1¾oz (50g) ball.

Debbie Bliss Cashmerino Aran:
* An aran-weight yarn.
* 55% merino wool, 33% microfiber, 12% cashmere.
* Approximately 99yd (90m)/1¾oz (50g)ball.

Debbie Bliss Cashmerino DK:
* A double-knitting-weight yarn.
* 55% merino wool, 33% microfiber, 12% cashmere.
* Approximately 120yd (110m)/1¾oz (50g) ball.

Debbie Bliss Cotton DK:
* A double-knitting-weight yarn.
* 100% cotton.
* Approximately 92yd (84m)/1¾oz (50g) ball.

Debbie Bliss Eco Baby:
* A fine-weight yarn.
* 100% organic cotton.
* Approximately 137yd (125m)/1¾oz (50g) ball.

Debbie Bliss Rialto Aran:
* An aran-weight yarn.
* 100% extra fine merino wool.
* Approximately 88yd (80m)/1¾oz (50g) ball.

Debbie Bliss Rialto DK:
* A double-knitting-weight yarn.
* 100% extra fine merino wool.
* Approximately 115yd (105m)/1¾oz (50g) ball.

Debbie Bliss Rialto Chunky:
* A chunky-weight yarn.
* 100% merino wool.
* Approximately 60m/1¾oz (50g) ball.

Debbie Bliss Riva:
* A chunky-weight yarn.
* 70% wool, 30% acrylic.
* Approximately 80m/1¾oz (50g) ball.

buying yarn
The yarn label carries all the essential information you need as to gauge, needle size, weight, and yardage. Importantly it will also have the dye-lot number. Yarns are dyed in batches or lots, which can vary considerably. As your retailer may not have the same dye lot later on, buy all your yarn for a project at the same time. If you know that sometimes you use more yarn than that quoted in the pattern, buy extra. If it is not possible to buy all the yarn you need with the same dye-lot number, use the different ones where it will not show as much, on a neck or border, as a change of dye lot across a main piece will most likely show.

It is also a good idea at the time of buying the yarn that you check the pattern and make sure that you already have the needles you will require. If not buy them now, as it will save a lot of frustration when you get home.

abbreviations
The abbreviations on the next page are standard ones. Any special abbreviations needed are provided at the beginning of the individual patterns.

Abbreviations

alt	alternate
beg	begin(ning)
cm	centimeter(s)
cont	continu(e)(ing)
dec	decreas(e)(ing)
foll	follow(s)(ing)
g	gram(s)
in	inch(es)
inc	increas(e)(ing)
k	knit
kfb	knit into front and back of next stitch
m	meter(s)
mm	millimeter(s)
M1	make one stitch by picking up loop lying between stitch just worked and next stitch and working into back of it
oz	ounce(s)
p	purl
patt	pattern; or work in pattern
psso	pass slipped stitch over
rem	remain(s)(ing)
rep	repeat(s)(ing)
skp	slip 1, knit 1, pass slipped stitch over
sl	slip
ssk	[slip 1 knitwise] twice, insert tip of left-hand needle from left to right through fronts of slipped stitches and k2tog
st(s)	stitch(es)
St st	stockinette stitch
tbl	through back loop(s)
tog	together
yd	yard(s)
yo	yarn over right needle to make a new stitch

Gift-wrapping Ideas

An exquisitely wrapped gift is a desirable object in itself, which only adds to the excitement of receiving a present. When you have taken so much care in hand knitting a present, don't lessen the impact by scrimping on the wrapping. With so many ready-made boxes and bags available, not to mention endless pretty ribbons, there really is no excuse not to create the perfect present.

A gift is a token of your love and esteem, so do take care to present it perfectly. There are so many stylish ways to wrap a present, but often simplicity is the best approach. I love the look and feel of plain brown parcel paper tied with raffia or string, then finished with a luggage label used as a gift tag. Recycling paper as gift-wrapping can look good as well as being eco conscious; leftover scraps of decorative wallpaper, out-of-date maps, and even the prettily pink newspaper all make interesting gift-wrapping paper.

The foolproof method of gift-wrapping is, of course, to opt for one of the many ready-made gift boxes and bags. These can be a neat solution, although not always the most economical. Tissue paper is a good cost-effective choice, but you do need to use two or three sheets together for coverage. I always try to keep packs of colored tissue paper in the cupboard along with a selection of ribbons. If your gift is a garment or larger item,

make sure that the hand knit is neatly folded. Layer the project with tissue paper to prevent the knit from from creasing. I recommend using acid-free tissue paper as it will prevent any discoloration if the hand knit is stored in the paper for any length of time. Adding tissue paper is also a useful way of filling out a gift box as well as providing an extra shot of color.

If the gift I am giving uses any buttons as part the design, such as the Teapot Cozy Wrap on page 132, I like to include one or two extra buttons in the package just in case any get lost. So don't forget to add a couple of spares to your shopping list when you are collecting the materials needed to make the project.

Finally, remember to add the laundry instructions inside your parcel. Either save the yarn label and tuck it into the gift-wrapping or copy out the care information onto a pretty gift tag or card which the recipient can keep safe.

For Her

Beaded Clutch Bag

This elegant evening bag takes just a single ball of Baby Cashmerino to make, plus some inexpensive glass beads for added sparkle. Each bead is first threaded onto the yarn and then worked into the knitted fabric, creating a sophisticated chevron design. Although it's a deceptively simple project to make, whoever receives this bag cannot fail to be impressed.

size
Approximately 4¾in x 6¼in (12cm x 16cm)

materials
* 1 x 1¾oz (50g) ball of Debbie Bliss Baby Cashmerino in bright pink
* Pair of US size 3 (3.25mm) knitting needles
* Approximately 2oz (60g) of ⅛in (3mm) silver-lined clear glass embroidery beads
* One fine collapsible-eye beading needle
* 20in x 8½in (50cm x 20cm) of fabric for lining
* Iron-on fabric interlining

gauge
25 sts and 34 rows to 4in (10cm) square over unbeaded St st using US size 3 (3.25mm) needles.

abbreviations
PB (place bead) bring yarn to front of work between needles, slip next stitch purlwise, push bead close to work, take yarn to back of work between needles to work next stitch.
Also see page 13.

notes

* Before casting on, you need to thread the beads onto the yarn. If your beading needle is made from very fine gauge wire with a long collapsible eye, you can thread the beads directly onto the yarn. If you have to use a fine needle with a small eye, thread the needle with a length of sewing thread tied to form a loop, then thread the yarn through the loop, so the beads thread onto the sewing thread first, then onto the yarn.

* The beads need to have a center hole, large enough for two thicknesses of yarn to pass through, or you will not be able to thread the beads. You may find a few beads that have a slightly smaller center hole, this is due to a thicker than normal coating of silver and you will need to discard these, but you will have more than enough to complete the bag.

* When working the back of the bag, turn the chart upside down as you will be repeating the chart from the 52nd to the 1st row.

to make (worked in one piece)

Front flap

With US size 3 (3.25mm) needles, cast on 45 sts.

1st row (right side) (1st chart row) K2, [PB, k1] to last st, k1.

2nd and all wrong-side rows P all sts, making sure beads sit on the right side of work.

3rd row K1, [PB, k1] to end.

Continue to work from chart until all 52 rows have been worked.

Foldline row (right side) P to end.

Back

Work from chart from 52nd to 1st row (see Notes), so ending with a right-side row.

Base

P 5 rows.

Front

Next row (right side) Work across 1st chart row.

Cont to work from chart from 2nd to 49th row, so ending with a right-side row.

Bind off knitwise on wrong side.

lining

Iron interlining onto wrong side of lining fabric. Using the knitted piece as a template, cut a piece of fabric, adding 5/8in (1.5cm) all around for seams. Fold seam allowance onto wrong side and press. Hand sew lining to wrong side of knitted piece.

to finish

Fold the piece along the base and sew bag front to bag back along the side edges, allowing front flap to fold onto right side.

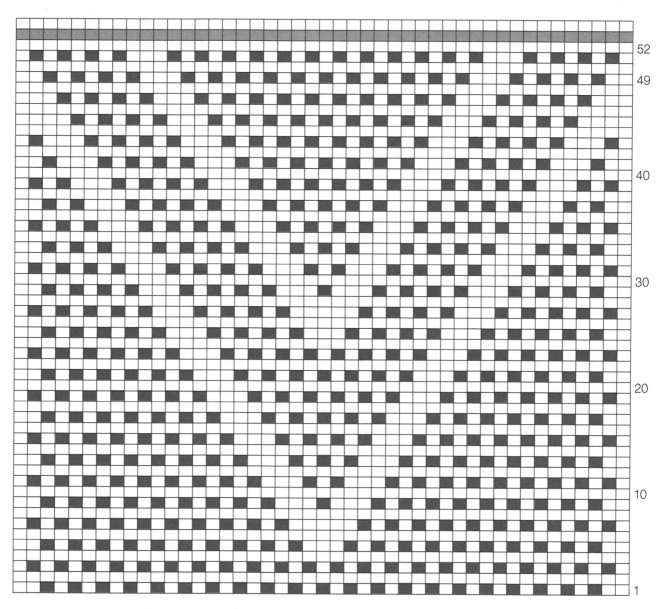

52
49
40
30
20
10
1

Key

☐ K on right-side rows and p on wrong-side rows

■ PB place bead—see abbreviations on page 19

▨ Foldline row—p on right side

Covered Bangles

If you are short on time but still want to give a handcrafted gift, these covered bangles are a satisfyingly quick knit. I have used three of my favorite texture stitches—seed stitch, blackberry stitch, and cables with bobbles—to make a tonally harmonious trio. Included in the instructions are tips on how to adjust the sizing of the knitted pieces to fit your preferred bangles, big or small.

size
Knitted cover fits ready-made bangle.

materials
Cable and bobble bangle
✶ 1 x 1¾oz (50g) ball of Debbie Bliss Baby Cashmerino in camel
✶ Pair of US size 3 (3.25mm) knitting needles
✶ One 1¼in (3cm) wide ready-made bangle with a circumference of 11in (28cm)

Seed stitch bangle
✶ 1 x 1¾oz (50g) ball of Debbie Bliss Rialto Aran in ecru
✶ Pair of US size 6 (4mm) knitting needles
✶ One 1¼in (3cm) wide ready-made bangle with a circumference of 11in (28cm)

Blackberry stitch bangle
✶ 1 x 1¾oz (50g) ball of Debbie Bliss Rialto Aran in chocolate
✶ Pair of US size 7 (4.5mm) knitting needles
✶ One 1½in (4cm) wide ready-made bangle with a circumference of 11in (28cm)

gauge
It is not essential to work to an exact gauge. See page 27 for how to adjust size.

abbreviations
MB [kfb] twice into next st, turn, p4, turn, k4, turn, [p2tog] twice, turn, k2tog.

T5R slip next 3 sts onto cable needle and hold at back of work, k2, then work [p1, k2] from cable needle.

C3BP slip next st onto cable needle and hold at back of work, k2, then p1 from cable needle.

C3FP slip next 2 sts onto cable needle and hold to front of work, p1, then k2 from cable needle.

Also see page 13.

note

* You can cover any size bangle, but if yours is wider or narrower than the ones here, you will need to adjust the number of stitches. The blackberry stitch and seed stitch bangles are worked to a length to fit the bangle, so any size can be worked, but with the cable and bobble bangle you may need to adjust the number of pattern repeats worked.

cable and bobble bangle

With US size 3 (3.25mm) needles, cast on 19 sts.
1st row (right side) P7, T5R, p7.
2nd row K7, p2, k1, p2, k7.
3rd row P6, C3BP, p1, C3FP, p6.
4th row K6, p2, k3, p2, k6.
5th row P5, C3BP, p3, C3FP, p5.
6th row K5, p2, k5, p2, k5.
7th row P5, k2, p2, MB, p2, k2, p5.
8th row Rep 6th row.
9th row P5, C3FP, p3, C3BP, p5.
10th row Rep 4th row.
11th row P6, C3FP, p1, C3BP, p6.
12th row Rep 2nd row.
These 12 rows **form** the pattern and are repeated 6 times more.
Bind off.

to finish

Sew cast-on edge to bound-off edge to make a circle. Place around bangle.
Sew row ends (sides) together, then slide around the bangle so the seam lies inside.

seed stitch bangle

With US size 6 (4mm) needles, cast on 13 sts.
Seed st row K1, [p1, k1] to end.
Rep this row until strip fits around the outside circumference of bangle when slightly stretched.
Bind off.

to finish

Work as Cable and Bobble Bangle.

blackberry stitch bangle

With US size 7 (4.5mm) needles, cast on 14 sts.
1st row (right side) Purl.
2nd row K1, * [k1, p1, k1] into next st, p3tog; rep from * to last st, k1.
3rd row Purl.
4th row K1, * p3tog, [k1, p1, k1] into next st; rep from * to last st, k1.
These 4 rows **form** the pattern and are repeated until strip fits around the outside circumference of bangle.
Bind off.

to finish

Work as Cable and Bobble Bangle.

Lacy Stole

This show-stopping stole would make such a special gift for a landmark birthday, anniversary, or other significant event. In striking magenta pink, the stole makes a statement accessory suitable for a glamorous evening out, but if knitted up in a more neutral shade it could be worn more casually as a wrap over fall weekends or curled up at home through winter nights.

size
Approximately 29in x 66in (74cm x 168cm)

materials
* 10 x $\frac{7}{8}$oz (25g) balls of Debbie Bliss Angel in magenta
* Pair of US size 8 (5mm) knitting needles

gauge
18 sts and 23 rows to 4in (10cm) square over St st using US size 8 (5mm) needles.

abbreviations
See page 13.

main piece

With US size 8 (5mm) needles, cast on 132 sts.
K 3 rows.
Work in patt as follows:
1st row K3, [skp, yo, k1, yo, k4, k2tog] to last 3 sts, k3.
2nd and every foll wrong-side row K3, p to last 3 sts, k3.
3rd row K3, [skp, k1, yo, k1, yo, k3, k2tog] to last 3 sts, k3.
5th row K3, [skp, k2, yo, k1, yo, k2, k2tog] to last 3 sts, k3.
7th row K3, [skp, k3, yo, k1, yo, k1, k2tog] to last 3 sts, k3.
9th row K3, [skp, k4, yo, k1, yo, k2tog] to last 3 sts, k3.
11th row K3, p to last 3 sts, k3.
12th row K to end.
These 12 rows **form** the pattern and are repeated.
Cont in patt until stole measures approximately 65½in (167cm) from cast-on edge, ending with a 9th row.
K 3 rows.
Bind off.

border

With US size 8 (5mm) needles, cast on 10 sts.
K 1 row.

Work in patt as follows:
1st row K1, k2tog, yo, k3, [yo, k2tog] twice.
2nd row Yo, k1, yo, k2tog, yo, k7. *12 sts.*
3rd row K1, k2tog, yo, k5, [yo, k2tog] twice.
4th row Yo, k1, yo, k2tog, yo, k9. *14 sts.*
5th row K1, k2tog, yo, k7, [yo, k2tog] twice.
6th row Yo, k1, yo, k2tog, yo, k11. *16 sts.*
7th row K1, k2tog, yo, k9, [yo, k2tog] twice.
8th row Yo, k2tog, [yo, k2tog], twice, k10.
9th row K1, k2tog, yo, k6, [k2tog, yo] twice, k3tog. *14 sts.*
10th row Yo, k2tog, [yo, k2tog], twice, k8.
11th row K1, k2tog, yo, k4, [k2tog, yo] twice, k3tog. *12 sts.*
12th row Yo, k2tog, [yo, k2tog], twice, k6.
13th row K1, k2tog, yo, k2, [k2tog, yo] twice, k3tog. *10 sts.*
14th row Yo, k2tog, [yo, k2tog], twice, k4.
These 14 rows **form** the pattern and are repeated.
Cont in patt until border fits along one side of stole, ending with a 14th row.
P 1 row.
Bind off.

to finish

Sew straight edge of edging to one side of stole.

Pillbox Hat

Diamonds may be considered a girl's best friend, but to my mind pearls make an equally desirable gift. This screen-siren-inspired pillbox hat is liberally peppered with pearl beads, which contrast strikingly against the bright red yarn. Using a milliner's sinamay pillbox base to provide the structure, the hat is knitted in stockinette stitch with simple decreases for the crown shaping.

size
To fit a pillbox hat base with a circumference of approximately 20in (51cm)

materials
* 1 x 1¾oz (50g) ball of Debbie Bliss Baby Cashmerino in red
* Pair of US size 3 (3mm) knitting needles
* One US size 3 (3mm) circular knitting needle
* Piece of lining fabric, 8in (20cm) in diameter
* One sinamay pillbox base with a circumference of approximately 20in (51cm)
* 24in (60cm) of 1½in (4cm) wide grosgrain ribbon
* 100 x ⅜in (10mm) pearl beads
* Approximately 16in (40cm) of hat elastic

gauge
27 sts and 36 rows to 4in (10cm) square over St st using US size 3 (3mm) needles.

abbreviations
See page 13.

to make

With US size 3 (3mm) needles, cast on 6 sts.

1st row (right side) K1, [kfb] to last st, k1. *10 sts.*

2nd and every wrong-side row P to end.

3rd row [Kfb] to last st, k1. *19 sts.*

5th row [K1, kfb] to last st, k1. *28 sts.*

7th row [K2, kfb] to last st, k1. *37 sts.*

9th row [K3, kfb] to last st, k1. *46 sts.*

Change to US size 3 (3mm) circular knitting needle.

Cont to inc 9 sts in this way on every right-side row, working one more st before each inc as set until there are 145 sts, ending with the last inc row.

Beg with a p row, work even in St st for 3¼in (8cm) more, ending with a p row.

Bind off.

to finish

Sew seam.

Place the circle of lining fabric inside the hat base and baste around the edge.

Place the knitted piece over the outside of the hat base and tack stitch to hold in place—the last row of shaping should match the top edge of the hat base. Fold the edge of the knitted piece inside the hat base and stitch in place, through the lining fabric and onto the base.

Using waxed thread (it is less likely to break than sewing thread), sew the pearl beads randomly over the outside of the hat.

Sew the hat elastic to the hat, securing it in place.

Stitch one edge of the ribbon around the inside of the hat, folding the end under to neaten, and covering the edge of the knitted piece.

Cabled Arm Warmers

Fingerless mittens worked in chunky pure merino yarn are both a practical and sumptuous present. The generous rib cuff is designed to bridge the usual gap between coat sleeve and glove, while the open ends leave fingers free to garden or even to knit. The simple yet effective "staghorn" cable running the length of the mittens is a good place for newcomers to cable knitting to start.

measurements
To fit average-size woman's hands

materials
* 2 x 1¾oz (50g) balls of Debbie Bliss Rialto Chunky in camel
* Pair of US size 10½ (6.5mm) knitting needles
* Cable needle

gauge
15 sts and 21 rows to 4in (10cm) square over St st using US size 10½ (6.5mm) needles.

abbreviations
C4B slip next 2 sts onto cable needle, hold at back of work, k2, then k2 from cable needle.
C4F slip next 2 sts onto cable needle, hold to front of work, k2, then k2 from cable needle.
Also see page 13.

to make (make two, both alike)

With US size 10½ (6.5mm) needles, cast on 38 sts.

1st row (right side) P2, [k2, p2, k2, p3] to end.

2nd row [K3, p2, k2, p2] to last 2 sts, k2.

These 2 rows **form** the rib and are repeated.

Work 3 rows more in rib.

Inc row [K3, p2, M1, k2, M1, p2] to last 2 sts, k2. *46 sts.*

Cont in patt as follows:

1st row (right side) P2, [k8, p3] to end.

2nd row [K3, p8] to last 2 sts, k2.

3rd row P2, [C4B, C4F, p3] to end.

4th row [K3, p8] to last 2 sts, k2.

These 4 rows **form** the cable pattern and are repeated.

Patt 6 rows more.

Dec row (right side) P2, [C4B, C4F, p2tog, p1] to end. *42 sts.*

Work 5 rows more in patt as now set.

Dec row P2, [k8, p2tog] to end. *38 sts.*

Work 3 rows more in patt as now set.

Thumb shaping

Next row Patt 19, M1, p1, M1, patt 18.

Work 1 row.

Next row Patt 19, M1, p3, M1, patt 18.

Work 1 row.

Next row Patt 19, M1, p5, M1, patt 18.

Work 1 row.

Next row Patt 19, M1, p7, M1, patt 18.

Work 1 row.

Next row Patt 19, M1, p9, M1, patt 18. *48 sts.*

Work 1 row.

Divide for thumb

Next row Patt 30, turn, cast on 3 sts.

Next row K14, turn.

Next row K2, [p2, k2] 3 times.

Next row P2, [k2, p2] 3 times.

Next row K2, [p2, k2] 3 times.

Bind off in rib.

Sew seam.

With right side facing, rejoin yarn to base of thumb, pick up and k one st, patt to end. *38 sts.*

Work 9 rows in patt.

Bind off in patt.

Sew seam.

Ribbon-Tied Belt

This elegant cabled knitted strip is finished with the finest grosgrain ribbon tied in a bow to create a gorgeous belt. The ribbon ties at the back make the belt fully adjustable, while the extra row of crochet along each long edge helps the belt to sit neatly around the waist. Experiment with different colorways; use either coordinating or clashing ribbons.

size
Approximately 26in (66cm) long (excluding ribbon)

materials
* 1 x 1¾oz (50g) ball of Debbie Bliss Bella in silver
* Pair of US size 5 (3.75mm) knitting needles
* US size D/3 (3.25mm) crochet hook
* 1yd (1m) of ⅝in (15mm) wide striped grosgrain ribbon

gauge
22 sts and 30 rows to 4in (10cm) square over St st using US size 5 (3.75mm) needles.

note
If you are working a longer belt, you will need one more 1¾oz (50g) ball of Debbie Bliss Bella.

abbreviations
C4B slip next 2 sts onto cable needle and hold at back of work, k2, then k2 from cable needle.
C4F slip next 2 sts onto cable needle and hold to front of work, k2, then k2 from cable needle.
C4BP slip next 2 sts onto cable needle and hold at back of work, k2, then p2 from cable needle.
C4FP slip next 2 sts onto cable needle and hold to front of work, p2, then k2 from cable needle.
Cr6L slip next 2 sts onto cable needle and hold to front of work, p2, k2, then k2 from cable needle.
Cr6R slip next 4 sts onto cable needle and hold at back of work, k2, then p4 from cable needle.
Also see page 13.

to make

With US size 5 (3.75mm) needles, cast on 20 sts.

1st row (right side) P1, k2, p2, k2, p6, k2, p2, k2, p1.

2nd row K1, p2, k2, p2, k6, p2, k2, p2, k1.

3rd–12th rows Rep 1st and 2nd rows 5 times more.

13th row P1, k2, p2, Cr6L, C4BP, p2, k2, p1.

14th, 16th, 18th, 20th, 22nd, and 24th rows (wrong side) K1, p2, k4, p6, k4, p2, k1.

15th, 19th, and 23rd rows P1, k2, p4, k2, C4B, p4, k2, p1.

17th and 21st rows P1, k2, p4, C4F, k2, p4, k2, p1.

25th row P1, k2, p2, Cr6R, C4FP, p2, k2, p1.

26th row K1, p2, k2, p2, k6, p2, k2, p2, k1.

These 26 rows **form** the pattern and are repeated 7 times more, then work 1st–11th rows once more.

Bind off in patt.

edging

With US size D/3 (3.25mm) crochet hook and working from the wrong side, work 1sc into every alternate st and row-end around the edges of the knitted strip. Fasten off.

to finish

Cut the ribbon into two pieces and folding ¾in (2cm) at one end of each piece, sew this end in place to the center 6-st section at each end of the knitted strip.

For Him

Rice Stitch Scarf

Textural rice stitch—so called because the little bumps look like grains of rice—makes a fine alternative to seed stitch, but it is just as simple to knit. Rice stitch is the perfect choice for a scarf as, unlike stockinette stitch, the side edges lay flat rather than roll inwards. Adapt the accent yarns that tip the scarf ends to suit the recipient; they could even reflect his favorite team colors.

size
Approximately 6in x 60in (15cm x 152cm)

materials
* 3 x 1¾oz (50g) balls of Debbie Bliss Rialto Aran in dark gray (A) and a small amount in each of fuchsia (B) and rust (C)
* Pair of US size 8 (5mm) knitting needles

gauge
22 sts and 24 rows to 4in (10cm) square over patt using US size 8 (5mm) needles.

abbreviations
See page 13.

to make

With US size 8 (5mm) needles and B, cast on 33 sts.

1st row (wrong side) P1, [k1tbl, p1] to end.

2nd row Knit.

These 2 rows **form** the pattern and are repeated.

Work 4 rows more in patt.

Change to A and cont in patt until scarf measures 59in (150cm) from cast-on edge, ending with a wrong-side row.

Change to C and patt 6 rows.

Bind off in patt.

Fingerless Gloves

Whether he is out gardening, dog walking, or goal keeping, the man in your life is sure to put to good use these practical fingerless gloves. Needing just a single ball of each color yarn, this is an economic project to give as a gift. At one end the long ribbed cuffs keep wrists cozy, while at the other end the two-row stripes are echoed in the playful alternating of red and green fingers.

size
To fit medium-size man's hands

materials
✳ 1 x 1¾oz (50g) ball each of Debbie Bliss Rialto DK in green (A) and maroon (B)
✳ Pair each of US size 3 (3.25mm) and US size 5 (3.75mm) knitting needles

gauge
23 sts and 31 rows to 4in (10cm) square over St st using US size 5 (3.75mm) needles.

abbreviations
See page 13.

right glove

** With US size 3 (3.25mm) needles and B, cast 48 sts.

Rib row [K1, p1] to end.

Rib 1 more row.

Change to A.

Rib 32 rows more.

Change to US size 5 (3.75mm) needles and beg with a k row, work in St st.

Cont in stripes of 2 rows B and 2 rows A.

Work 6 rows. **

Thumb shaping

Next row K25, M1, k1, M1, k22.

Work 3 rows.

Next row K25, M1, k3, M1, k22.

Work 3 rows.

Next row K25, M1, k5, M1, k22.

Work 3 rows.

Next row K25, M1, k7, M1, k22.

Work 3 rows.

Next row K25, M1, k9, M1, k22. *58 sts.*

Work 3 rows, ending with 2 rows B.

Divide for thumb

Next row K37 in A, turn, cast on 3 sts.

Next row P16 in A.

Work 12 rows in St st in A only.

Bind off.

With right side facing and A, pick up and k 3 sts from base of thumb, k to end. *48 sts.*

Work 13 rows in stripe sequence, so ending 2 rows A.

*** **First finger**

Next row K30 in B, turn and cast on 2 sts.

Next row P15 in B, turn, cast on 2 sts.

Cont in B only and work 10 rows in St st.

Bind off.

Sew seam.

Second finger

With right side facing and B, pick up and k 2 sts from base of first finger, k6, turn, cast on 2 sts.

Next row P15, turn, cast on 2 sts.

Change to A and work 12 rows St st.

Bind off.

Sew seam.

Third finger

With right side facing and B, pick up and k 2 sts from base of second finger, k6, turn, cast on 2 sts.

Next row P15, turn, cast on 2 sts.

Cont in B only and work 10 rows in St st.

Bind off.

Sew seam.

Fourth finger

With right side facing and B, pick up and k 2 sts from base of third finger, k6, turn.

Next row P15.

Change to A and work 6 rows St st.

Bind off.

Sew seam.

left glove

Work as given for Right Glove from ** to **.

Thumb shaping

Next row K22, M1, k1, M1, k25.

Work 3 rows.

Next row K22, M1, k3, M1, k25.

Work 3 rows.

Next row K22, M1, k5, M1, k25.

Work 3 rows.

Next row K22, M1, k7, M1, k to end.

Work 3 rows.

Next row K22, M1, k9, M1, k to end. *58 sts.*

Work 3 rows, so ending 2 rows B.

Divide for thumb

Next row K34 in A, turn cast on 3 sts.

Next row P16 in A.

Cont in A only and work 12 rows St st.

Bind off.

With right side facing and A, pick up and k 3 sts from base of thumb, k to end. *48 sts.*

Work 13 rows in stripe sequence, so ending 2 rows A.

Complete as for Right Glove from *** to end.

Walking Socks

Everyone deserves a touch of luxury in their life. These aran socks ensure happy feet, even when he is digging in the garden or hiking across hills. The perfect pair of long socks to slip into gardening or walking boots, this design incorporates contrast color heels and toes, plus a striped rib top. You only need a small amount of each, so use up leftover yarns for these accent colors.

size
To fit men's shoe size US 10–11

materials
* 4 x 1¾oz (50g) balls of Debbie Bliss Cashmerino Aran in plum (M) and 1 x 1¾oz (50g) ball in each of gold (A), royal (B), and tangerine (C)
* Set of four US size 7 (4.5mm) double-pointed knitting needles

gauge
20 sts and 26 rows to 4in (10cm) square over St st using US size 7 (4.5mm) needles.

abbreviations
See page 13.

to make

With US size 7 (4.5mm) needles and A, cast on 64 sts.
Arrange these sts on 3 needles and cont in rounds.

Rib round [K2, p2] to end.

This round **forms** the rib and is repeated.

Work 1 round more.

Cont in rib in stripes of 2 rows each of [B, C, M, and A] twice, then 2 rows B and 2 rows C.

Cont in rib in M only until work measures 17¾in (45cm) from cast-on edge.

Dec round [K2, p2tog] to end. *48 sts.*

Cut yarn.

Divide sts onto 3 needles as follows: slip first 12 sts onto first needle, next 12 sts onto second needle, next 12 sts onto 3rd needle, then slip last 12 sts onto other end of first needle.

Shape heel

With right side facing, join A to 24 sts on first needle and work in rows on these 24 sts only.

Beg with a k row, work 13 rows in St st.

Shape heel

** **Next row** Sl 1, p to end.

Next row Sl 1, k13, skp, k1, turn.

Next row Sl 1, p5, p2tog, p1, turn.

Next row Sl 1, k6, skp, k1, turn.

Next row Sl 1, p7, p2tog, p1, turn.

Next row Sl 1, k8, skp, k1, turn.

Next row Sl 1, p9, p2tog, p1, turn.

Next row Sl 1, k10, skp, k1, turn.

Next row Sl 1, p11, p2tog, p1, turn.

Next row Sl 1, k12, skp, turn.

Next row Sl 1, p12, p2tog, turn. *14 sts.*

Cut yarn.

Foot shaping

With right side facing and M, k14, pick up and k 11 sts along side of back heel, k1, place a marker, k 22 sts from needles, place a marker, k1, pick up and k 11 sts along other side of back heel. *60 sts.*

Arrange these sts evenly on 3 needles and cont in rounds as follows:

1st round K to within 3 sts of marker k2tog, k1, slip marker, k to next marker, slip marker, k1, skp, k to end.

2nd round K to end.

Rep the last 2 rounds 5 times more. *48 sts.*

Slipping markers on every round, work even until sock measures 8¼in (21cm) from back of heel.

Change to B.

Shape toe

1st round K to within 3 sts of marker k2tog, k1, slip marker, k1, skp, k to within 3 sts of next marker, k2tog, k1, slip marker, k1, skp, k to end.

2nd round K to end.

Rep the last 2 rounds until 24 sts rem.

Slip first 6 sts onto one needle, next 12 sts onto a second needle, then slip rem 6 sts onto other end of first needle.

Transfer the two groups of sts onto safety pins, fold sock inside out, then transfer the sts back onto two needles and bind off one st from each needle together.

Make second sock exactly the same.

iPad™ Cover

Tweed and leather are a classic combination, fit for every discerning gentleman. This cover for an original iPad™ or other tablet device is made from robust cotton knitted into a hardwearing tweed stitch fabric secured with fine leather ties. The pinstripe lining adds a splash of color: you could always recycle a favorite shirt to personalize the present.

size
Approximately 26in (66cm) long (excluding ribbon) to closely fit an original iPad™

materials
* 1 x 1¾oz (50g) ball of Debbie Bliss Bella in chocolate
* Pair of US size 8 (5mm) knitting needles
* Piece of fine cotton fabric 10¾in x 21¼in (27cm x 54cm) for lining
* 1yd (1m) of ⅝in (15mm) wide leather strip or ribbon

gauge
23 sts and 38 rows to 4in (10cm) square over tweed st using US size 8 (5mm) needles.

abbreviations
yb take yarn to back of work between two needles.
yf bring yarn to front of work between two needles.
Sl 1p slip 1 st purlwise.
Also see page 13.

To make

With US size 8 (5mm) needles, cast on 59 sts.

1st row (wrong side) K1, [yf, sl 1p, yb, k1] to end.

2nd row (right side) P2, [yb, sl 1p, yf, p1] to last st, p1.

These 2 rows **form** the tweed st patt and are repeated throughout.

Work in patt until piece measures 7½in (19cm), ending with a wrong-side row.

Place a marker at each end of last row.

Cont in patt and cast on 2 sts at beg of next 2 rows. *63 sts.*

Cont in patt until piece measures 19in (48cm) from original cast-on edge, ending with a right-side row.

Bind off knitwise.

To finish

Sew approximately ¾in (2cm) of one end of the leather or ribbon strip to the wrong side of the knitted piece, placing it centrally behind the bound-off edge.

Fold ½in (1cm) all around the edge of the fabric lining onto the wrong side and press in place. Slipstitch the fabric to the wrong side of the knitted piece, placing it centrally, so the 2 sts at each side that were cast on for the gusset remain unlined.

Fold the piece across the width where the 2 sts are cast on at each side. Sew the cast-on sts at each side to the row ends below the fold, so forming a small gusset, then continue to sew together the row ends down to the cast-on edge.

Seed Stitch Tie

I just love the combination of cherry red yarn and my all-time favorite seed stitch to make this tie. I've made it long enough to be tied into an old-fashioned windsor knot, however, if you want to make a smaller tie for a youngster, simply knit a shorter strip. Why not present the tie in a gift box along with step-by-step illustrations on how to tie a knot correctly, which can be easily found online?

size
56in (142cm) long

materials
* 2 x 1¾oz (50g) balls of Debbie Bliss Baby Cashmerino in red
* Pair each of US size 2 (2.75mm) and US size 3 (3.25mm) knitting needles
* 15in (38cm) of 1in (2.5cm) wide grosgrain ribbon

gauge
28 sts and 48 rows to 4in (10cm) square over seed st using US size 3 (3.25mm) needles.

abbreviations
See page 13.

To make

With US size 3 (3.25mm) needles, cast on 13 sts.

Seed st row K1, [p1, k1] to end.

This row **forms** seed st and is repeated throughout.

Cont in seed st until strip measures 26in (66cm) from cast-on edge.

Place markers at each end of last row.

Change to US size 2 (2.75mm) needles.

Cont in seed st for 4 rows more.

Dec row K1, [p1, k1] twice, p3tog, [k1, p1] twice, k1. *11 sts.*

Cont in seed st until strip measures 40½in (103cm) from cast-on edge.

Place markers at each end of last row.

Change to US size 3 (3.25mm) needles.

Cont in seed st until strip measures 56in (142cm) from cast-on edge.

Bind off in seed st.

To finish

Neaten ribbon by folding ⅝in (1.5cm) at each end onto wrong side and stitch folds
in place.

Stitch ribbon to wrong side of tie centrally between markers. If preferred, you can also
fold the edges of the cast-on and bound-off edges onto the wrong side to make points
at each end of the tie. Position the ribbon-backed section of the tie around the neck to
lie under the collar, before tying.

Houndstooth Dog Jacket

As a dedicated dog lover, I simply couldn't resist including a gift for Man's Best Friend! Whether pedigree or pooch, no dog could fail to look dapper in this houndstooth check. The instructions given here are suited for a medium-sized breed, such as my own Beagle, Monty, but the jacket is held in place using elastic and hook-and-loop fastener for both adaptability and ease.

size
To fit a medium-sized dog

materials
* 2 x 1¾oz (50g) balls of Debbie Bliss Rialto Aran in black (A) and 1 x 1¾oz (50g) ball in red (B)
* Pair of US size 7 (4.5mm) knitting needles
* ⅝in (1.5cm) piece of ¾in (2cm) wide sew-on hook-and-loop fastener (Velcro®)
* Approximately 25½in (65cm) of ¾in (2cm) wide elastic

gauge
23 sts and 24 rows to 4in (10cm) square over patterned St st using US size 7 (4.5mm) needles.

abbreviations
See page 13.

note
Written instructions are given for the overall shape of the jacket, but the chart is used to place the 4-stitch, 4-row houndstooth pattern.

houndstooth pattern

Worked over 4 sts.

1st row (right side) K1A, k1B, k2A.

2nd row P3B, p1A.

3rd row K3B, k1A.

4th row P1A, p1B, p2A.

These 4 rows **form** the check pattern and are repeated.

to make

With US size 7 (4.5mm) needles and A, cast on 70 sts.
Beg with a k row, work in St st and placing the pattern
as shown on the chart on page 71, shape as follows:
Work 4 rows.

Next row (right side) Kfb, k to last 2 sts, kfb, k1.

P 1 row.

Rep the last 2 rows 3 times more. *78 sts.*

Work even for 8 rows.

Next row (right side) Skp, k to last 2 sts, k2tog.

Work 3 rows.

Rep the last 4 rows 5 times more. *66 sts.*

Work even for 20 rows.

Next row (right side) Kfb, k to last 2 sts, kfb, k1.

Work 3 rows.

Rep these 4 rows 3 times more. *74 sts.*

Shape neck

Next row (right side) K26, turn and cont on these sts
only, leave rem sts on a spare needle.

Bind off 2 sts at beg (neck edge) of next row and 3 foll
wrong-side rows. *18 sts.*

K 1 row.

Next row (wrong side) P2tog, p to end.

Work 6 rows.

Next row Skp, k to last 2 sts, k2tog.

P 1 row.

Rep the last 2 rows twice more.

Next row Skp, k to end.

P 1 row.

Rep the last 2 rows once more. Bind off rem 9 sts.

With right side facing, rejoin A to sts on spare needle,
bind off 22 sts, patt to end. P 1 row.

Bind off 2 sts at beg (neck edge) of next row and 3 foll
right-side rows. *18 sts.*

P 1 row.

Next row (right side) Skp, k to end.

Work 5 rows.

Next row Skp, k to last 2 sts, k2tog.

P 1 row.

Rep the last 2 rows twice more.

Next row Skp, k to end.

P 1 row.

Rep the last 2 rows once more. Bind off rem 9 sts.

Press on wrong side.

edging

With US size 7 (4.5mm) needles and A, cast on 5 sts.

Seed st row K1, [p1, k1] twice.

This row is repeated throughout.

Work in seed st until strip fits around the edge of the jacket,
allowing extra to accommodate the corners and neck edge.
Do not bind off, leave the sts on a holder and do not cut
the yarn, this will enable you to either add or subtract
more rows if necessary.

to finish

Working through the edge st of the edging, sew in place
around the jacket, easing around the corners and neck
edge. Bind off the 5 sts and sew together the ends.

Sew one piece of hook-and-loop fastener to the neck
edging—the loop on the right side of the right front neck
and the hook on the wrong side of the left front neck, to
fasten around the dog's neck.

Put the jacket onto the dog and fasten at the neck, mark
the position for the elastic, then remove the jacket. Fold
½in (1cm) at each end of the elastic onto the wrong side
and sew the folds in place. Sew one end of the elastic to
the wrong side of the edging at the right-hand side of the
jacket. Sew the remaining piece of hook-and-loop fastener
to the elastic and the edging—the hook to the elastic and
the loop to the edging on the left-hand side of the jacket;
the elastic goes under the dog to hold the jacket in place.

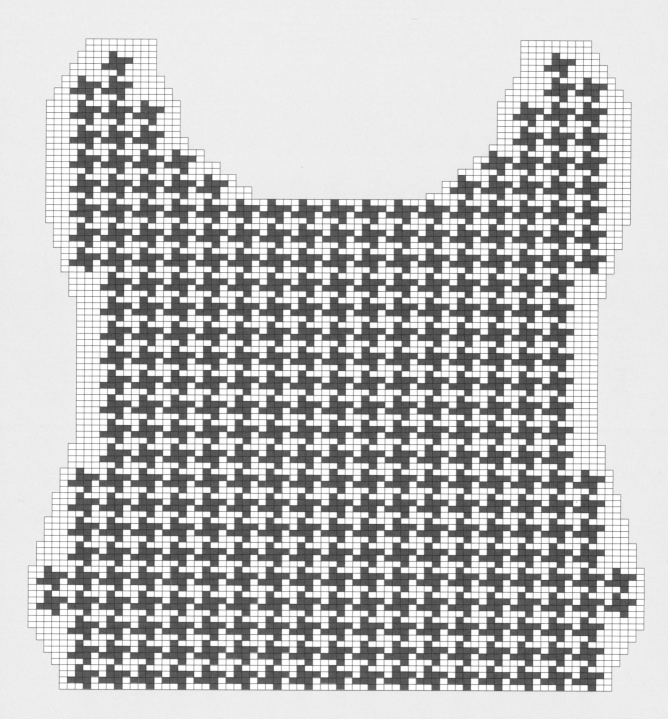

Key

☐ A

■ B

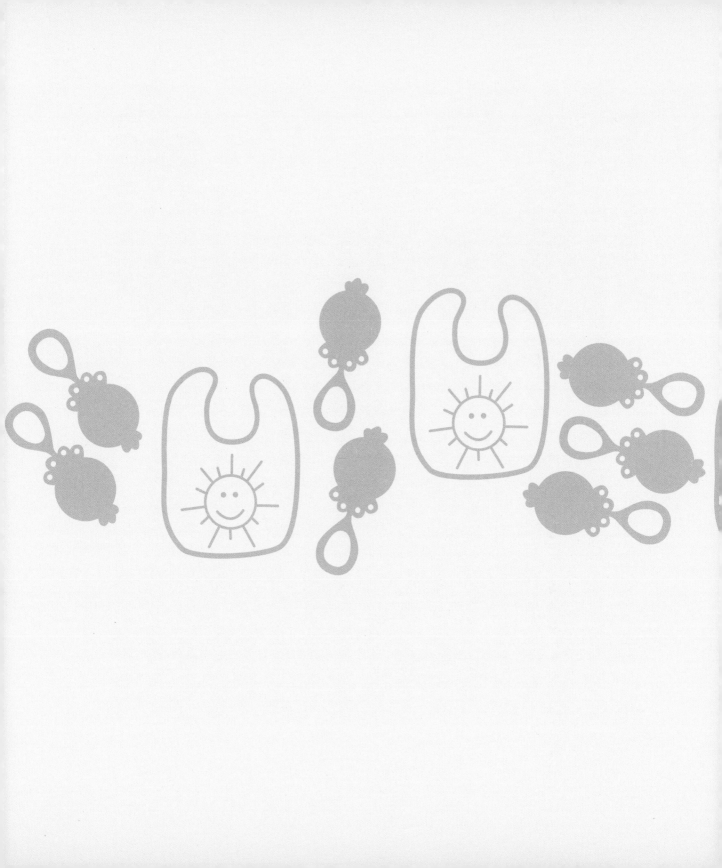

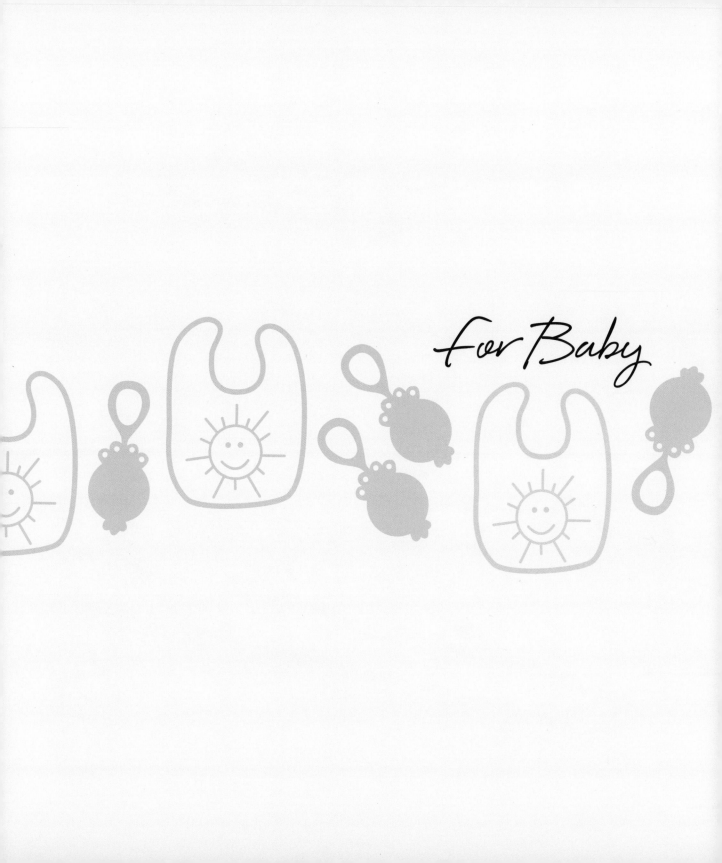

For Baby

Baby Shawl

Pretty enough for a special Christening gift, yet cozy enough for everyday use, this baby's shawl is the perfect way to welcome a precious newborn into the world. The relief of the embossed leaf stitch design works just as well in other pale pastel shades or even classic white. Guaranteed to melt any new parent's heart, this shawl will become an instant family heirloom.

size
Approximately 27½in x 33½in (70cm x 85cm)

materials
* 10 x 1¾oz (50g) balls of Debbie Bliss Baby Cashmerino in pale pink
* One US size 3 (3.25mm) circular knitting needle

gauge
25 sts and 34 rows to 4in (10cm) square over St st using US size 3 (3.25mm) needles.

abbreviations
See page 13.

to make

With US size 3 (3.25mm) needles, cast on 182 sts.

P 1 row.

Work in patt as follows:

1st row P2, [k9, k3tog, yo, k1, yo, p2] to end.

2nd and every foll wrong-side row K2, [p13, k2] to end.

3rd row P2, [k7, k3tog, k1, yo, k1, yo, k1, p2] to end.

5th row P2, [k5, k3tog, k2, yo, k1, yo, k2, p2] to end.

7th row P2, [k3, k3tog, k3, yo, k1, yo, k3, p2] to end.

9th row P2, [yo, k1, yo, sl 1, k2tog, psso, k9, p2] to end.

11th row P2, [k1, yo, k1, yo, k1, sl 1, k2tog, psso, k7, p2] to end.

13th row P2, [k2, yo, k1, yo, k2, sl 1, k2tog, psso, k5, p2] to end.

15th row P2, [k3, yo, k1, yo, k3, sl 1, k2tog, psso, k3, p2] to end.

16th row K2, [p13, k2] to end.

These 16 rows **form** the pattern and are repeated.

Cont in patt until work measures 33½in (85cm) from cast-on edge, ending with a 15th patt row.

Next row P to end.

Bind off.

Bunny Booties

Who could resist this cute pair of bunnies, with their long floppy ears and twitchy noses. Perhaps best of all, these booties can be made using just one ball of Debbie Bliss Cashmerino DK yarn in the main color, plus small amounts for the pompon tail and embroidery details. They will keep a young baby's toes cozy, before they become a toddler and start hopping about themselves.

size
To fit age 3–6 months

materials
* 1 x 1¾oz (50g) ball of Debbie Bliss Cashmerino DK in each of duck egg blue (A) and ecru (B) and a small amount of chocolate yarn for embroidery
* Pair of US size 3 (3.25mm) knitting needles

gauge
25 sts and 34 rows to 4in (10cm) square over St st using US size 3 (3.25mm) needles.

abbreviations
See page 13.

main part (make 2)

With US size 3 (3.25mm) needles and A, cast on 36 sts.
K 5 rows.
Beg with a k row, work 7 rows in St st.
K 2 rows.
Rib row [K1, p1] to end.
Rep the rib row 9 times more and inc 3 sts evenly across
last row. *39 sts.*
Beg with a k row, work 4 rows in St st.

Shape instep

Next row K26, turn.
Next row P13, turn.
Work 13 rows in St st on these 13 sts only.
Next row P3, [p2tog, p3] twice.
Cut yarn.
With right side facing, rejoin yarn at base of instep,
pick up and k 8 sts along side edge of instep, k 11 sts of
instep, pick up and k 8 sts along other side of instep,
k rem 13 sts. *53 sts.*
Beg with a p row, work 14 rows in St st.
Next row [P next st tog with corresponding st 7 rows
below] to end.

Shape sole

Next row Sl first 21 sts onto right-hand needle, rejoin
yarn and k10, k2tog, turn.
Next row Sl 1, k9, k2tog tbl, turn.
Next row Sl 1, k9, k2tog, turn.
Rep last 2 rows 8 times more, then work first of the
2 rows again.
Next row Sl 1, k3, sl 1, k2tog, psso, k3, k2tog, turn.
Next row Sl 1, k7, k2tog tbl, turn.
Next row Sl 1, k7, k2tog, turn.
Rep last 2 rows once more, then work first of the
2 rows again.

Next row Sl 1, k2, sl 1, k2tog, psso, k2, k2tog, turn.
Next row Sl 1, k5, k2tog tbl, turn.
Next row Sl 1, k5, k2tog, turn.
Rep last 2 rows 3 times more.
Next row Sl 1, k2, k2tog, k1, k2tog tbl.
Place rem sts at each side of sole on one needle, with
the needle point in same direction as the needle with
sole sts. With right sides together and taking one st from
each needle each time, bind off rem sts together.

outer ears (make 4)

With US size 3 (3.25mm) needles and A, cast on 7 sts.
Beg with a k row, work 12 rows in St st.
Next row K1, [k2tog, k1] twice.
Work 3 rows.
Next row K2tog, k1, k2tog.
Next row Work 3tog and fasten off.

inner ears (make 4)

With US size 3 (3.25mm) needles and B, cast on 5 sts.
Beg with a k row, work 12 rows in St st.
Next row K2tog, k1, k2tog.
Work 3 rows.
Next row Work 3tog and fasten off.

to finish

Sew back seam of main part of each bootie, reversing
seam on cuff. Turn back cuff. Sew inner ears to outer
ears. Fold in half at cast-on edge and stitch together first
4 rows of outer layers. Sew ears in place, and embroider
eyes and nose with chocolate yarn.

Seed Stitch Overalls

These smart dungarees are deceptively easy to make but are sure to be a hugely appreciated gift. Knitted in my favorite seed stitch, with rib cuffs and bib, only minimal shaping is required. If you don't want to tackle a buttonhole, simply add a large snap instead. Either way, the practical shoulder fastenings make it easy to slip the overalls on and off a wriggling child.

measurements

To fit ages

0–3	3–6	6–9	9–12	months

Finished measurements

Around chest

19¾	21¼	23¼	25½	in
50	54	59	64	cm

Length to shoulder (adjustable)

16½	17¾	19	20	in
42	45	48	51	cm

Inside leg length

4	4¼	4¾	5	in
10	11	12	13	cm

materials

* 4(5:5:6) x 1¾oz (50g) balls of Debbie Bliss Baby Cashmerino in faded blue
* Pair each of US size 2 (2.75mm) and US size 3 (3.25mm) knitting needles
* 2 buttons

gauge

26 sts and 44 rows to 4in (10cm) square over seed st using US size 3 (3.25mm) needles.

abbreviations

yo2 yarn over right needle twice to make 2 stitches.
Also see page 13.

back

First leg

With US size 2 (2.75mm) needles, cast on 32(34:36:38) sts.

Rib row [K1, p1] to end.

Rep the last row 7 times more.

Change to US size 3 (3.25mm) needles.

1st seed st row (right side) [K1, p1] to end.

2nd seed st row [P1, k1] to end.

These 2 rows **form** the seed st.

Inc row (right side) Inc in first st, seed st to end.

Work 3 rows.

Rep the last 4 rows 6(7:8:9) times more and the inc row again. *40(43:46:49) sts.*

Work even until leg measures 4(4¼:4¾:5)in/ 10(11:12:13)cm, ending with a wrong-side row.

Shape crotch

Next row (right side) Bind off 4 sts, patt to end. *36(39:42:45) sts.*

Patt 1 row.

Leave these sts on a holder.

Second leg

With US size 2 (2.75mm) needles, cast on 32(34:36:38) sts.

Rib row [K1, p1] to end.

Rep the last row 7 times more.

Change to US size 3 (3.25mm) needles.

1st seed st row (right side) [P1, k1] to end.

2nd seed st row [K1, p1] to end.

These 2 rows **form** the seed st.

Inc row (right side) Patt to last 2 sts, inc in next st, patt last st.

Work 3 rows.

Rep the last 4 rows 6(7:8:9) times more and the inc row again. *40(43:46:49) sts.*

Work even until leg measures 4(4¼:4¾:5)in/ 10(11:12:13)cm, ending with a right-side row.

Shape crotch

Next row (wrong side) Bind off 4 sts, patt to end. *36(39:42:45) sts.*

Patt 1 row.

Next row Patt 35(38:41:44), work last st tog with first st of left leg, patt 35(38:41:44). *71(77:83:89) sts.*

Next row Patt to end.

Next row Patt 34(37:40:43), work 3 tog, patt 34(37:40:43).

Patt 15 rows.

Next row Patt 33(36:39:42), work 3 tog, patt 33(36:39:42).

Patt 15 rows.

Next row Patt 32(35:38:41), work 3 tog, patt 32(35:38:41). *65(71:77:83) sts.*

Work even until back measures 10¾(11½:12¼:13)in/ 27(29:31:33)cm from cast-on edges, ending with a wrong-side row.

Next row P1, [k1, p1] to end.

Next row K1, [p1, k1] to end.

Rep the last 2 rows 7 times more.

Shape armholes

Bind off 6(8:8:10) sts at beg of next 2 rows.
53(55:61:63) sts.

Next row K2, [p1, k1] to last 3 sts, p1, k2.

Next row K1, [p1, k1] to end. **

Rep the last 2 rows until armhole measures
3¼(3½:4:4¼)in/8(9:10:11)cm, ending with a wrong-
side row.

Shape back neck

Next row K2, [p1, k1] 3(3:4:4) times, p1, k2, turn and
work on these sts only for first strap.

Next row K1, [p1, k1] to end.

Next row K2, [p1, k1] to last st, k1.

Cont in rib as set until strap measures 4in (10cm),
ending with a wrong-side row.

Bind off in rib.

With right side facing, rejoin yarn to rem sts, bind off
center 31(33:35:37) sts, with one st on needle after
bind-off, [k1, p1] 4(4:5:5) times, k2.

Next row K1, [p1, k1] to end.

Next row K2, [p1, k1] to last st, k1.

Work on these sts in rib as set, until strap measures
4in (10cm), ending with a wrong-side row.

Bind off in rib.

front

Work as given for Back to **.

Rep the last 2 rows until armhole measures
1½(2:2¼:2¾)in/4(5:6:7)cm , ending with a wrong-
side row.

Shape front neck

Next row K2, [p1, k1] 3(3:4:4) times, p1, k2, turn and
work on these sts for first strap.

Next row K1, [p1, k1] to end.

These 2 rows **form** the rib.

1st buttonhole row Rib 3(3:4:4), work 2 tog, yo2, work
2 tog, rib to end.

2nd buttonhole row Rib to end, working twice into yo2.

Work 8 rows more.

Bind off in rib.

With right side facing, rejoin yarn to rem sts, bind off
center 31(33:35:37) sts, with one st on needle after
bind-off, [k1, p1] 4(4:5:5) times, k2.

Next row K1, [p1, k1] to end.

1st buttonhole row Rib 4(4:5:5), work 2 tog, yo2, work
2 tog, rib to end.

2nd buttonhole row Rib to end, working twice into yo2.

Work 8 rows more.

Bind off in rib.

to finish

Sew together inner leg and side seams. Try the overalls
on the baby and mark the position for the buttons on the
back straps. Sew on buttons to match markers.

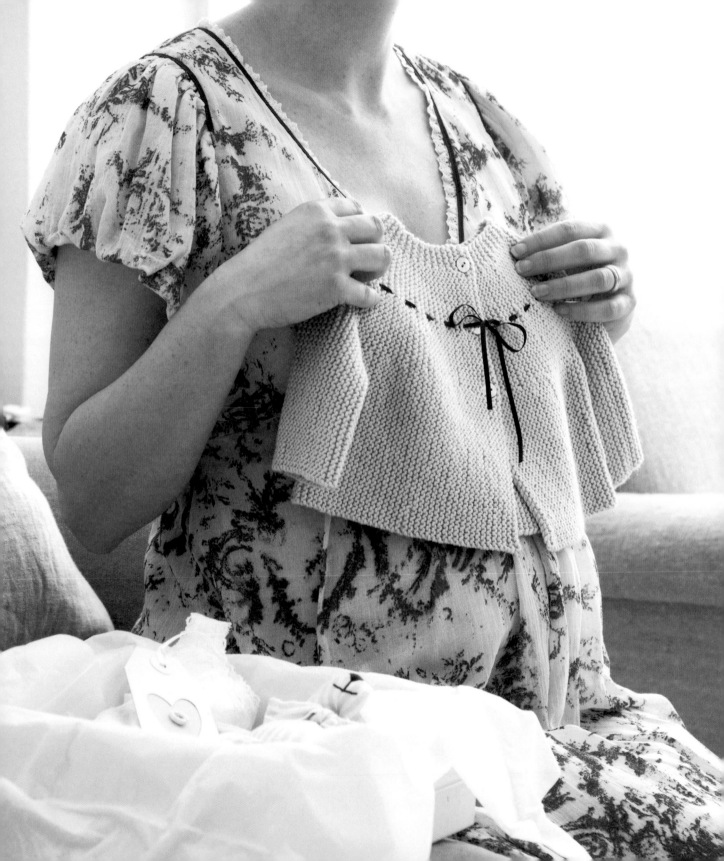

Garter Stitch Jacket

Handmade gifts will always be treasured, whatever they are. The time invested in creating something unique is a reflection of the maker's feelings. Preparing for parenthood is an extra-special time and many mothers-to-be like to share this moment with their family and friends by throwing a baby shower. This elegant baby jacket, knitted all in one piece, couldn't be a more perfect present.

measurements

To fit ages

0–3	3–6	6–9	months

Finished measurements

Around chest

18	19¾	21¼	in
46	50	54	cm

Length to back neck

8¾	10	11	in
22	25	28	cm

Sleeve length

4¼	5½	6½	in
11.5	14	16.5	cm

materials

* 3(4:4) x 1¾oz (50g) balls of Debbie Bliss Baby Cashmerino in pale gray (M)
* Pair of US size 3 (3.25mm) knitting needles
* 3 buttons
* 1yd (1m) of narrow ribbon

gauge

25 sts and 50 rows to 4in (10cm) square over garter st using US size 3 (3.25mm) needles.

abbreviations

See page 13.

to make (worked in one piece)

Left front

With US size 3 (3.25mm) needles, cast on 55(63:71) sts.
K 5 rows (for button band).

** Next 2 rows K29(35:41), turn, k to end.

Next 2 rows K40(47:54), turn, k to end.

Next 2 rows K51(59:67), turn, k to end.

K 2 rows across all 55(63:71) sts. **

Rep from ** to ** 8(9:10) times more.

Next row K29(35:41), turn and cont on these sts only,
leave rem 26(28:30) sts on a holder for yoke.

K 5 rows.

Leave these 29(35:41) sts on a holder for back.

Left sleeve

With US size 3 (3.25mm) needles, cast on 29(35:41) sts.
K 5 rows.

Working across 29(35:41) sts of sleeve and 26(28:30)
sts of yoke; rep from ** to ** 7(8:9) times.

Next row K29(35:41), turn and cont on these sts only,
leave 26(28:30) sts of yoke on a holder.

K 5 rows.

Bind off.

Back

Return to 29(35:41) sts of back on holder.

K 6 rows.

Working across 29(35:41) sts of back and 26(28:30) sts
of yoke, rep from ** to ** 18(19:20) times.

Next row K29(35:41), turn and cont on these sts only,
leave rem 26(28:30) sts of yoke on a holder.

K 5 rows.

Leave these 29(35:41) sts on a holder for right front.

Right sleeve

Work as given for Left Sleeve.

Right Front

Return to 29(35:41) sts of right front on holder.

Work 6 rows.

Working across 29(35:41) sts of right front and 26(28:30)
sts of yoke, rep from ** to ** 9(10:11) times.

K 2 rows.

Buttonhole row K29(35:41), yo, k2tog, [k9(10:11), yo,
k2tog] twice, k2.

K 2 rows.

Bind off.

to finish

Using a flat seam, sew sleeve seams. Sew underarm
seam. Sew on buttons. Thread the ribbon around the
yoke, level with the center buttonhole as shown.

Sun Hat

During the warmer months young skin needs protection from the sun, so this floppy-brimmed hat is the ideal accessory to pack when heading off on your family summer vacation. Made with Debbie Bliss Eco Baby, this breathable cotton knit will help to keep baby cool. All you need is a single ball of the main shade of yarn, and leftover yarns for the contrasting picot edging.

measurements
To fit ages

| 0–3 | 3–6 | 6–9 | months |

materials
✳ 1 x 1¾oz (50g) ball of Debbie Bliss Eco Baby in pale green (A) and small amounts in duck egg blue (B) and aqua (C)
✳ Pair each of US size 3 (3.25mm) and US size 8 (5mm) needles

gauge
25 sts and 34 rows to 4in (10cm) square over St st using US size 3 (3.25mm) needles.

abbreviations
See page 13.

main part

With US size 3 (3.25mm) needles and A, cast on 92(101:110) sts.

Beg with a k row, work 24(26:28) rows in St st.

Shape crown

1st row [K8(9:10), k2tog] 9 times, k2. *83(92:101) sts.*

2nd row P to end.

3rd row [K7(8:9), k2tog] 9 times, k2.

4th row P to end.

5th row [K6(7:8), k2tog] 9 times, k2.

6th row P to end.

7th row [K5(6:7), k2tog] 9 times, k2.

8th row P to end.

9th row [K4(5:6), k2tog] 9 times, k2.

10th row P to end.

11th row [K3(4:5), k2tog] 9 times, k2.

12th row P to end.

13th row [K2(3:4), k2tog] 9 times, k2.

14th row P to end.

15th row [K1(2:3), k2tog] 9 times, k2. *20(29:38) sts.*

16th row P to end.

2nd and 3rd sizes only

17th row [K–(1:2), k2tog] 9 times, k2. *–(20:29) sts.*

18th row P to end.

3rd size only

19th row [K1, k2tog] 9 times, k2. *–(–:20) sts.*

20th row P to end.

All sizes

Next row [K2tog] 10 times.

Next row [P2tog] 5 times.

Leaving a long end, cut yarn, thread through rem sts, pull up, and secure.

brim

With right side facing, US size 3 (3.25mm) needles, and A, pick up and k 92(99:106) sts evenly along cast-on edge of main part.

Beg with a p row, work in St st.

Work 1 row.

1st inc row (right side) K1, [M1, k6(7:8), M1, k7] 7 times. *106(113:120) sts.*

Work 2 rows.

2nd inc row [P8, M1, p7(8:9), M1] 7 times, p1. *120(127:134) sts.*

Work 2 rows.

3rd inc row K1, [M1, k8(9:10), M1, k9] 7 times. *134(141:148) sts.*

Work 2 rows.

4th inc row [P10, M1, p9(10:11), M1] 7 times, p1. *148(155:162) sts.*

K 2 rows.

Edging

Change to B and beg with a k row, work 4 rows in St st.

Change to US size 8 (5mm) needles and C.

Picot row K1, [yo, k2tog] to end.

Change to US size 3 (3.25mm) needles and work 4 rows.

Bind off with US size 8 (5mm) needles.

to finish

Sew seam. Fold edging along picot row and slipstitch bound-off edge to the inside of the brim.

Zebra Toy

Inspired by the animals of the African savannahs, there is no mistaking this knitted zebra with his distinctive black and white stripes. With his luxurious mane and swishy tail, this handsome zebra is a welcome addition to any baby's toy shelf to sit alongside the more conventional teddy bears and dolls. You can even dress him up in a smart cotton apron trimmed with rickrack.

size
Approximate height 10in (25cm)

materials
* 1 x 1¾oz (50g) ball of Debbie Bliss Rialto DK in each of black (A) and ecru (B)
* Pair of US size 3 (3.25mm) knitting needles
* Washable toy stuffing (see Notes)
* 10in (25cm) of ribbon (optional)

gauge
25 sts and 56 rows to 4in (10cm) square over striped garter st using US size 3 (3.25mm) needles.

notes
* All parts are worked using US size 3 (3.25mm) needles.
* Worked in 2-row garter st stripes of A and B.
* Make sure you use a washable toy stuffing that is also nonflammable (flame retardant) and nontoxic and adheres to safety regulations.

* For optional apron, use rickrack and a fabric scrap. Follow the cutting guide below, edge with the rickrack, and use rickrack for straps and ties.

abbreviations
s2togkp slip next 2 sts tog knitwise, k1, then pass slipped sts over knit st. Also see page 13.

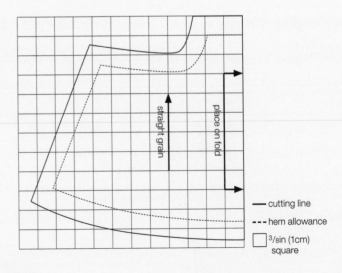

straight grain

place on fold

— cutting line
--- hem allowance
☐ ³⁄₈in (1cm) square

front legs (make 2)

Hoof

With A, cast on 4 sts.

Next row (right side) With A, [kfb] 3 times, k1. *7 sts.*

P 1 row A.

Next row With A, [k1, M1, k2, M1] twice, k1. *11 sts.*

Beg with a p row, work 2 rows St st in A.

Next row (wrong side) With A, p3, p2tog tbl, p1, p2tog, p3. *9 sts.*

Leg

K 2 rows B.

K 1 row A.

Next row (wrong side) With A, k3, [M1, k3] twice.

Beg with B and cont in garter st stripes of 2 rows B and 2 rows A, k 22 rows, so ending with a 2-row stripe in B.

Leave sts on a holder.

body front (worked from base upward)

With A, cast on 13 sts and k 1 row.

Next row (right side) With B, k6, M1, k1, M1, k6. *15 sts.*

K 1 row B.

K 2 rows A.

Next row With B, k7, M1, k1, M1, k7. *17 sts.*

K 1 row B.

K 2 rows A.

Beg with B, k 22 rows more in 2-row stripes, so ending with a B stripe.

Leave sts on the needle.

body back

Work exactly as given for Body Front.

upper body

With right side facing and A, k across 17 sts of Body Back, k 11 sts of Left Front Leg, k 17 sts of Body Front, k 11 sts of Right Front Leg. *56 sts.*

K 1 row A.

Next row With B, [ssk, k13, k2tog, ssk, k7, k2tog] twice. *48 sts.*

K 1 row B.

K 2 rows A.

Next row With B, [ssk, k3, ssk, k1, k2tog, k3, k2tog, ssk, k5, k2tog] twice. *36 sts.*

K 1 row B.

K 2 rows A.

Next row With B, [ssk, k1, ssk, k1, k2tog, k1, k2tog, ssk, k3, k2tog] twice. *24 sts.*

K 1 row B.

K 2 rows A.

Next row With B, [ssk, s2togkp, k2tog, ssk, k1, k2tog] twice. *12 sts.*

K 1 row B.

K 2 rows A.

Cut yarn, thread through rem 12 sts, pull up, and secure.

Sew together shaped edges of upper body, then continue to sew side seam.

Sew rem side seam, then sew front leg seams.

Stuff front legs and body with toy stuffing, leaving cast-on body edges open.

head

With A, cast on 5 sts.

Next row (right side) [Kfb] 4 times, k1. *9 sts.*

P 1 row.

Next row [K2, M1] twice, k1, [M1, k2] twice. *13 sts.*

P 1 row.

Now work in 2-row garter st stripes of B and A throughout as follows:

K 2 rows B.

Next row (right side) With A, k1, M1, k to last st, M1, k1. *15 sts.*

K 9 rows.

Next row K4, M1, k1, M1, k5, M1, k1, M1, k4. *19 sts.*

K 11 rows.

Next row K4, [ssk] twice, k3, [k2tog] twice, k4. *15 sts.*

K 1 row.

Next row K3, [ssk] twice, k1, [k2tog] twice, k3. *11 sts.*

K 1 row.

Next row K1, [ssk] twice, k1, [k2tog] twice, k1. *7 sts.*

Next row (wrong side) Ssk, s2togkp, k2tog. *3 sts.*

Cut yarn and thread through rem sts, pull up, and secure. Sew seam, leaving a small opening, stuff head lightly, and sew opening closed.

Work a few sts in A on the head for the eyes, then work a central stitch in B on each eye.

ears (make 2)
With A, cast on 3 sts.
K 2 rows.
Next row S2togkp and fasten off.
Sew ears in place to head.

back legs (make 2)
With A, cast on 8 sts and p 1 row.
Next row (right side) [Kfb] 7 times, k1. *15 sts.*
P 1 row.
Next row K1, M1, k4, [M1, k1] 6 times, k3, M1, k1. *23 sts.*
P 1 row.
Next row K9, k2tog, k1, ssk, k9. *21 sts.*
P 1 row.
Next row K8, k2tog, k1, ssk, k8. *19 sts.*
Next row P7, p2tog tbl, p1, p2tog, p7. *17 sts.*
Next row K7, s2togkp, k7. *15 sts.*
P 1 row.
Next row K5, k2tog, k1, ssk, k5. *13 sts.*
P 1 row.
Beg with 2 rows in B, k 44 rows in 2-row garter st stripes of B and A throughout.
Bind off.
Sew seam, leaving bound-off edges open. Stuff lightly. With seams at the back, sew legs together side by side at the top edge.

to finish
Position joined back legs inside the open edge of the body and stitch in place all around, so closing all open edges. Sew head in place on the body. Tie a piece of ribbon around the neck (optional).

For optional apron, see Notes on page 96.

tail
Make a braid with 6 strands of yarn, knot the end, and trim strand ends to tidy tail. Sew to the back of the body.

mane
Step 1
Thread a 3¼in (8cm) loop of yarn through the eye of the needle and insert the point of the needle from top to bottom through bar in the center of a stitch.

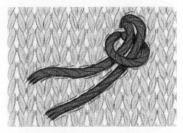

Step 2
Pull yarn loop through, then remove needle. Pass the 2 yarn ends through the loop.

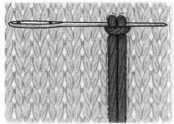

Step 3
Place the needle under the double yarn above the loop and pull the yarn ends to tighten the loop onto the yarn.

Repeat these steps working mane down the center back head and part way down the center back body, making sure the yarn is securely held in place so it can't be easily removed, you may need to add a couple of stitches in sewing thread to each tuft to make absolutely sure.

For Kids

Hair Band With Bow

There really couldn't be a simpler or speedier project to make, yet this sweet hair band with bow is extremely effective. Have fun mixing and matching different colors—I just love this combination of coral pink yarn and apple green ribbon. As an alternative to a hair band, you could always attach a brooch back to the reverse of the bow so it can then be pinned onto either a jacket or a bag.

size
To fit a child of any age as ribbon length is adjustable

materials
* 1 x 1¾oz (50g) ball of Debbie Bliss Eco Baby in coral
* Pair of US size 3 (3mm) knitting needles
* 1yd (1m) of ½in (1cm) wide ribbon (or length to suit)

gauge
It is not essential to work this bow to an exact gauge.

abbreviations
See page 13.

Main section

With US size 3 (3mm) needles, cast on 12 sts.

Work in garter st (k every row) until strip measures approximately 6¼in (16cm).

Bind off.

Sew cast-on and bound-off edges together.

Center band

With US size 3 (3mm) needles, cast on 6 sts.

Work in garter st (k every row) until strip measures approximately 2¾in (7cm).

Bind off.

Sew cast-on and bound-off edges together.

Making sure the seam lies in the center, pinch the middle of the main section, then slide the center band into position with the seam at the back. Thread the ribbon through the center band, behind the bow. Stitch the center band to the main section. Tie around the head.

Ladybug Backpack

With its unmistakeable red and black spotty wings, this backpack is transformed into a ladybug bag—perfect for carrying school books, playtime toys, or a packed lunch. When worn over the shoulders, the webbing straps become the ladybug's antenna. To carry on the spotted theme, I have lined the backpack with a printed cotton of black with red dots but any lining fabric will do.

size
11in (28cm) high and 9in (23cm) wide

materials
* 2 x 1¾oz (50g) balls of Debbie Bliss Rialto Aran in black (A) and 1 x 1¾oz (50g) ball in red (B)
* Pair each of US size 7 (4.5mm) and US size 8 (5mm) knitting needles
* ½yd (50cm) of cotton fabric for lining
* 10in (25cm) zipper
* 9in x 3¼in (23cm x 8cm) stiff cardboard
* Two 1in (2.5cm) black plastic side-release buckles with fixed bar
* Two 8in (20cm) pieces of 1in (2.5cm) wide black cotton webbing tape
* Two 16in (41cm) pieces of 1½in (38mm) wide black cotton webbing tape

gauge
18 sts and 24 rows to 4in (10cm) square over St st using US size 8 (5mm) needles.

abbreviations
See page 13.

base
With US size 7 (4.5mm) needles and A, cast on 68 sts.
K 1 row.
1st inc row (right side) K17, M1, k1, M1, k32, M1, k1, M1, k17.
K 1 row.
2nd inc row K17, M1, k3, M1, k32, M1, k3, M1, k17.
K 1 row.
3rd inc row K17, M1, k5, M1, k32, M1, k5, M1, k17.
K 1 row.
Cont to inc 4 sts in this way on 4 foll right-side rows, working two more k sts between each pair of increase sts, until there are 96 sts, ending with the 7th increase row.
K 1 row.
Change to US size 8 (5mm) needles.
Place chart on page 111 as follows:
Next row (right side) K27A, k across 42 sts of 1st row of chart, k27A.
Next row K2A, p25A, p across 42 sts of 2nd row of chart, p25A, k2A.

These 2 rows set the position of the chart in St st with 2 sts in garter st to each side.

Cont in this way until 48th chart row has been worked.

Next row (right side) With A, k22, ssk, k2tog, k1; k across 49th chart row; with A, k1, ssk, k2tog, k22. *92 sts.*

Next row With A, k2, p23; p across 50th chart row; with A, p23, k2.

Next row With A, k25; p across 51st chart row; with A, k25.

Next row With A, k2, p23; p across 52nd chart row; with A, p23, k2.

Next row With A, k21, ssk, k2tog; k across 53rd chart row; with A, ssk, k2tog, k21. *88 sts.*

Next row With A, k2, p21; p across 54th chart row; with A, p21, k2.

Next row With A, k20, ssk, k2tog; k across 40 sts of 55th chart row; with A, ssk, k2tog, k20. *84 sts.*

Next row With A, k2, p20; p across 40 sts of 56th chart row; with A, p20, k2.

Next row With A, k19, ssk, k2tog; k across 38 sts of 57th chart row; with A, ssk, k2tog, k19. *80 sts.*

Next row With A, k2, p19; p across 38 sts of 58th chart row; with A, p19, k2.

Next row With A, k18, ssk, k2tog; k across 36 sts of 59th chart row; with A, ssk, k2tog, k18. *76 sts.*

Next row With A, k2, p18; p across 36 sts of 60th chart row; with A, p18, k2.

Next row With A, k17, ssk, k2tog; k across 34 sts of 61st chart row; with A, ssk, k2tog, k17. *72 sts.*

Next row With A, k2, p17; p across 34 sts of 62nd chart row; with A, p17, k2.

Cont in A only and work as follows:

Divide for backs and front

Next row (right side) K16, ssk, turn and cont on these 17 sts for right back, leave rem sts on spare needle.

Next row P2tog tbl, p13, k2.

Next row K14, ssk.

Next row Slipping the first st, bind off 2 sts, p to last 2 sts, k2.

Next row K to end.

Rep the last 2 rows once more.

Next row Slipping the first st, bind off 3 sts, p to last 2 sts, k2.

Next row K to end.

Next row Slipping the first st, bind off 3 sts, p to last 2 sts, k2.

Next row K to end.

Bind off rem 5 sts.

With right side facing, rejoin yarn to sts on spare needle, k2tog, k32, ssk, turn and cont on these 34 sts only for back, leave rem sts on the spare needle.

Next row P2tog tbl, p to last 2 sts, p2tog.

Next row K2tog, k to last 2 sts, ssk.

Slipping the first st, bind off 2 sts at beg of next 4 rows, then bind off 3 sts at beg of foll 4 rows.

Bind off rem 10 sts.

With right side facing, rejoin yarn to sts on spare needle, k2tog, k to end.

Next row K2, p13, p2tog.

Next row K2tog, k to end.

Next row K2, p to end.

Next row Slipping the first st, bind off 2 sts, k to end.

Rep the last 2 rows once more.

Next row K2, p to end.

Next row Slipping the first st, bind off 3 sts, k to end.

Rep the last 2 rows once more. Bind off rem 5 sts.

to finish

Sew together row ends of base, then sew back opening for ½in (1cm). Sew together cast-on edge to complete base. Sew together top ½in (1cm) of back opening. Hand sew zipper in place behind open edges of back opening. Round off the corners of the cardboard to fit into the base of the bag. Using the cardboard as a template cut a piece of lining fabric, adding ⅝in (1.5cm) around the edge. Cut another piece of lining fabric about 21¾in x 12¼in (55cm x 31cm), fold in half to form a tube, and taking ⅝in (1.5cm) seams, stitch each end of the seam, leaving the center open for about 10in (25cm), to match the center back opening of the bag. Fold the base lining in

half and mark the center of one long side, then matching the seam of the fabric tube to the base marker, sew the base into the tube. Fold the lining in half with the seam centrally placed and sew across the top of the lining, rounding the corners.

Hem both ends of each length of tape, then assemble the two pieces of narrower tape in the pronged end of the side-release buckles. Sew end of each tape to the right side of the bag just above the base edge. Sew one end of each of the wider tapes to the wrong side of the

bag back, either side of the center back seam, angling the tape so the two pieces form a V shape. Folding the free end of each tape, assemble them into the other half of the side-release buckles and stitch firmly in place. Sew the shaped edges of the top of the bag in place, so completing the bag shape and enclosing the tapes. Insert the cardboard base into the bag and if necessary, hold in place by working a few sts through the cardboard and the bag. Insert the lining into the bag and slipstitch the opening edge to the zipper tape.

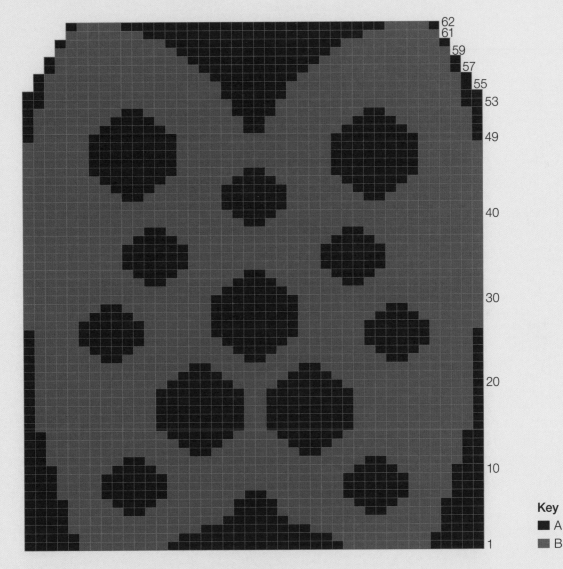

Key
■ A
■ B

Party Shrug

Every little girl looks pretty in pink. This slip-on shrug in a deep shade of coral mohair is the perfect partywear—teamed with a floaty dress it really does make an outfit fit for a princess. Made in an unconventional way, there is no back or front to be knitted for this shrug: the bound-off edges of both sleeves are joined to make the center back seam and the rib edging provides the collar.

measurements

To fit ages

2/3	3/4	4/5	years

Finished measurements

Across back

12½	14¼	15¾	in
32	36	40	cm

Length to center back neck (including border)

6¾	7½	8¼	in
17	19	21	cm

Sleeve length (with cuff turned back)

6¾	7½	8¼	in
17	19	21	cm

materials

* 2(2:3) x ⅞oz (25g) balls of Debbie Bliss Angel in coral
* Pair each of US size 3 (3.25mm), US size 6 (4mm), and US size 7 (4.5mm) knitting needles

gauge

22 sts and 30 rows to 4in (10cm) square over St st using US size 6 (4mm) needles.

abbreviations

See page 13.

right sleeve

With US size 6 (4mm) needles, cast on 42(50:58) sts.

1st rib row K2, [p2, k2] to end.

2nd rib row P2, [k2, p2] to end.

Rep the last 2 rows 10 times more. Place markers at each end of last row to indicate foldline.

Change to US size 3 (3.25mm) needles.

Work 22 rows in rib.

Change to US size 6 (4mm) needles. Beg with a k row, work even in St st until sleeve measures 6¾(7½:8¼)in/ 17(19:21)cm from foldline markers, ending with a p row. **

Shape top of sleeve

Next row K3, skp, k to end.

Place a second marker at beg of last row for start of Back.

Next row P to end.

Rep the last 2 rows 8 times more. *33(41:49) sts.*

Next row K3, skp, k to end.

Next row P to last 5 sts, p2tog tbl, p3.

Rep the last 2 rows 5(7:9) times more. *21(25:29) sts.*

Work even for 18(20:22) rows. Bind off.

left sleeve

Work as given for Right Sleeve to **.

Shape top of sleeve

Next row K to last 5 sts, k2tog, k3.

Place a marker at end of last row for start of Back.

Next row P to end.

Rep the last 2 rows 8 times more. *33(41:49) sts.*

Next row K to last 5 sts, k2tog, k3.

Next row P3, p2tog, p to end.

Rep the last 2 rows 5(7:9) times more. *21(25:29) sts.*

Work even for 18(20:22) rows. Bind off.

left front border and collar

With right side of left sleeve facing and US size 6 (4mm) needles, pick up and k 18(24:30) sts along straight back neck edge from end of bound-off edge to start of raglan shaping, and 32(34:36) sts along raglan edge. *50(58:66) sts.*

1st row P2, [k2, p2] to end. This row **sets** the rib.

Next 2 rows Rib 10(14:18), turn, rib to end.

Next 2 rows Rib 14(18:22), turn, rib to end.

Next 2 rows Rib 18(22:26), turn, rib to end.

Next 2 rows Rib 22(26:30), turn, rib to end.

Cont in this way working 4 extra sts on every right-side row until all sts have been worked, ending with a wrong-side row. Work 2 rows in rib across all sts.

** Inc row (right side) K2, [p2, k1, M1, k1] to last 4 sts, p2, k2. *61(71:81)sts.*

Change to US size 7 (4.5mm) needles.

Next row P2, [k2, p3] to last 4 sts, k2, p2.

Next row K2, [p2, k3] to last 4 sts, p2, k2.

The last 2 rows re-set the rib.

Rib 13 rows more across all sts. Bind off loosely in rib. **

right front border and collar

With right side of right sleeve facing and US size 6 (4mm) needles, pick up and k 32(34:36) sts along raglan edge then 18(24:30) sts along straight back neck edge to end of bound-off edge. *50(58:66) sts.*

Work in rib as set for Left Front Border and Collar.

Next 2 rows Rib 10(14:18), turn, rib to end.

Next 2 rows Rib 14(18:22), turn, rib to end.

Next 2 rows Rib 18(22:26), turn, rib to end.

Next 2 rows Rib 22(26:30), turn, rib to end.

Cont in this way working 4 extra sts on every right-side row until all sts have been worked, ending with a right-side row. Work 3 rows in rib across all sts.

Work as given for Left Front Border and Collar from ** to **.

lower back border

Join back seam (bound-off sleeve edges) and collar seam, reversing last 4in (10cm) of collar seam.

With right side facing and US size 6 (4mm) needles, pick up and k 78(86:94) sts between both second markers.

1st row (wrong side) P2, [k2, p2] to end.

2nd row K2, [p2, k2] to end.

Rep the last 2 rows 8 times more and the first row again. Bind off in rib.

To finish, sew sleeve and border seams.

Lion Cub Scarf

For the youngest member of your own pride, make this lion cub
scarf with a huge amount of character. The knitting is divided
to make a slot at one end, then the other end of the scarf is fed
through this opening so that it will sit neatly and securely in place
around the neck, even when your cub is running wild across the
plains...or playground.

size
To fit a child of any age

materials
* 3 x 1¾oz (50g) balls of Debbie Bliss
Rialto DK in caramel (A) and 1 x 1¾oz (50g)
ball in each of orange (B), ecru (C), and
black (D)
* Pair of US size 5 (3.75mm) knitting
needles

gauge
24 sts and 33 rows to 4in (10cm) square
over St st using US size 5 (3.75mm)
needles.

abbreviations
See page 13.

head back

With US size 5 (3.75mm) needles and B, cast on 9 sts.
Beg with a k row, work in St st throughout.
Work 2 rows.
3rd row Cast on 2 sts, k these sts, k to last st, M1, k1. *12 sts.*
4th row Cast on 2 sts, p these sts, p to last st, M1. *15 sts.*
5th row K1, M1, k to last st, M1, k1. *17 sts.*
6th row P1, M1, p to last st, M1, p1. *19 sts.*
Work 2 rows.
9th row K1, M1, k to last st, M1, k1. *21 sts.*
Work 9 rows.
19th row K1, M1, k to last st, M1, k1. *23 sts.*
Work 3 rows.
23rd row K1, M1, k to last st, M1, k1. *25 sts.*
Work 1 row.
25th row K1, M1, k to last st, M1, k1. *27 sts.*
26th row P1, M1, p to last st, M1, p1. *29 sts.*
Work 2 rows.
29th row K1, M1, k to last st, M1, k1. *31 sts.*
Work 3 rows.
33rd row K1, M1, k to last st, M1, k1. *33 sts.*
Work 2 rows.
36th row P1, M1, p to last st, M1, p1. *35 sts.*
37th row K1, M1, k to last st, M1, k1. *37 sts.*
Work 1 row.
39th row K1, M1, k to last st, M1, k1. *39 sts.*
Work 4 rows.
44th row P2tog, p to last 2 sts, p2tog tbl. *37 sts.*
45th row Ssk, k to last 2 sts, k2tog. *35 sts.*
46th row P2tog, p7, turn, leave rem sts on the needle.
Next row Ssk, k4, k2tog.
Bind off rem 6 sts, slipping the first st and working last 2 sts tog while binding off.
With wrong side facing, rejoin yarn to rem 26 sts, bind off 17 sts, p to last 2 sts, p2tog tbl. *8 sts.*
Next row Ssk, k4, k2tog.
Bind off rem 6 sts, slipping the first st and working last 2 sts tog while binding off.

face

With US size 5 (3.75mm) needles and B, cast on 9 sts.
Beg with a k row, work in St st from chart throughout, the shaping is worked in the same way as Head Back.

scarf

With US size 5 (3.75mm) needles and A, cast on 60 sts.
1st row (right side) [K1, p1] to end.
2nd row [P1, k1] to end.
Rep these 2 rows once more.
Next row K1, p1, k27, p1, k1, p1, k27, p1.
Next row P1, k1, p27, k1, p1, k1, p27, k1.
These 2 rows **form** the pattern and are repeated.
Work 20 rows more in patt.
Place markers at each end of last row.
Divide for opening
Next row (right side) K1, p1, k27, p1, turn and cont on these 30 sts only, leave rem sts on a holder.
Next row P1, k1, p27, k1.
Patt 19 rows more on these 30 sts, so ending with a right-side row.
Leave these sts on a spare needle or holder.
With right side facing, rejoin yarn to 30 sts on first holder, k1, p1, k27, p1.
Cont in patt on these 30 sts for 20 rows more, so ending with a right-side row.
Joining row (wrong side) Patt across 30 sts on needle, then patt across 30 sts on holder. *60 sts.*
Place markers at each end of last row.
Cont in patt until scarf measures 20¾in (53cm), ending with a wrong-side row.
Next row [K1, p1, k11, ssk, k2tog, k12, p1] twice. *56 sts.*
Patt 5 rows.
Next row [K1, p1, k10, ssk, k2tog, k11, p1] twice. *52 sts.*
Patt 5 rows.
Next row [K1, p1, k9, ssk, k2tog, k10, p1] twice. *48 sts.*
Patt 5 rows.
Cont to dec 4 sts in next row and every foll 6th row until 28 sts rem.
Work even in patt until scarf measures 28in (71cm) from

cast-on edge, ending with a wrong-side row.
Now work 3 rows in seed st across all sts.
Bind off in seed st.

to finish
Join Face and Head Back together around all edges.
Fold scarf in half lengthwise and sew together row ends,
leaving an opening in the seam between markers. Refold
scarf so the seam is central and sew together the cast-
on edge from fold to fold. Match up central opening with
opening in seam and sew together around the edge.
Position cast-on edge of scarf behind head and sew in
place, making sure, the opening lies just above the head.
Place around neck and thread the narrower end of scarf
from front to back through the opening and pull through.

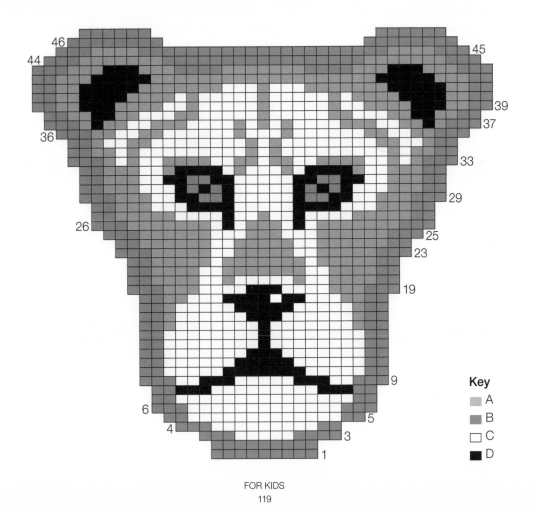

Key
■ A
■ B
□ C
■ D

Stripey Long Socks

Who says socks have to be a matching pair? As you can see, for a quirky touch, the striped color bands are ever so slightly different on the right and left socks. They are knitted in the round on a set of four needles, but don't let that intimidate you. Once you get started, you'll soon get the hang of it. And the best part of all is that once you have finished knitting, there are no seams to sew.

size
To fit ages

4–6   6–8   years

materials
✳ 3 x 1¾oz (50g) balls of Debbie Bliss Baby Cashmerino in gray (M) and 1 x 1¾oz (50g) ball in each of bright green (A), fuchsia (B), terracotta (C), and turquoise (D)
✳ Set of four US size 3 (3.25mm) double-pointed knitting needles
✳ Two safety pins

gauge
25 sts and 34 rows to 4in (10cm) square over St st using US size 3 (3.25mm) needles.

abbreviations
See page 13.

stripe sequence for first sock

4 rows M, 6 rows A, 4 rows M, 14 rows B, 4 rows M, 4 rows C, 4 rows M, 10 rows D.

These 50 rows **form** the stripe patt and are repeated.

stripe sequence for second sock

4 rows M, 6 rows D, 4 rows M, 14 rows A, 4 rows M, 4 rows B, 4 rows M, 10 rows C.

These 50 rows **form** the stripe patt and are repeated.

to make

With US size 3 (3.25mm) needles and M, cast on 80(88) sts.

Distribute sts evenly on 3 needles.

Work in correct stripe patt and rib as follows:

1st round [K1, p1] to end.

This round **forms** the rib and is repeated.

Work even until sock measures 12(14)in/30(35)cm, ending after 2 rows in M.

Cont in M only.

Next round [Skp] to end. *40(44) sts.*

Cont in St st and work in rows not rounds.

Back heel shaping

1st row K9(10) turn.

2nd row Sl 1, p17(19), turn.

3rd row Sl 1, k17(19), turn.

Work on these 18(20) sts, arrange rem 22(24) sts on two needles.

Rep the last 2 rows 8 times more, ending with a k row.

Shape heel

** **Next row** Sl 1, p to end.

Next row Sl 1, k9(11), skp, k1, turn.

Next row Sl 1, p3(5), p2tog, p1, turn.

Next row Sl 1, k4(6), skp, k1, turn.

Next row Sl 1, p5(7), p2tog, p1, turn.

Next row Sl 1, k6(8), skp, k1, turn.

Next row Sl 1, p7(9), p2tog, p1, turn.

Next row Sl 1, k8(10), skp, turn.

Next row Sl 1, p8(10), p2tog, turn. *10(12) sts.*

Foot shaping

With right side facing, k10(12), pick up and k 12 sts along side of back heel, k0(1), place a marker, k 22(22) sts from needles, place a marker, k0(1), pick up and k 12 sts along other side of back heel. *56(60) sts.*

Arrange these sts evenly on 3 needles and cont in rounds as follows:

1st round K to within 3 sts of marker, k2tog, k1, slip marker, k to next marker, slip marker, k1, skp, k to end.

2nd round K to end.

Rep the last 2 rounds 7 times more. *40(44) sts.*

Slipping markers on every round, work even until foot measures 5½(6)in/14(15)cm from ** or until work fits from back of heel to beg of toes.

Shape toe

1st round K to within 3 sts of marker k2tog, k1, slip marker, k1, skp, k to within 3 sts of next marker, k2tog, k1, slip marker, k1, skp, k to end.

2nd round K to end.

Rep the last 2 rounds until 20(20) sts rem.

Slip first 5 sts onto one needle, next 10 sts onto another needle and rem and 5 sts onto end of first needle.

Transfer the two groups of sts onto safety pins, fold sock inside out, then transfer the sts back onto two needles and bind off one st from each needle together.

Cabled Vest

An extremely useful cabled vest with a wide neck, so it can be easily popped over young heads without any struggle. The stripe in the ribbed waistband and armhole cuffs is continued in the ribbed cowl collar. I have knitted it up in toning shades of mid and light blue, but this vest would look equally great in white with a navy trim—perfect for a trip to the seaside.

---

measurements

To fit ages

3–6	6–9	9–12	12–18	18–24	months

Finished measurements

Around chest

17¾	19	20½	22	24	in
45	48	52	56	61	cm

Length to shoulder

8¾	9½	10¼	11	11¾	in
22	24	26	28	30	cm

materials

✳ 2(2:3:3:3) x 1¾oz (50g) balls of Debbie Bliss Baby Cashmerino in teal (A) and 1 x 1¾oz (50g) ball in light blue (B)
✳ Pair each of US size 2 (2.75mm) and US size 3 (3.25mm) knitting needles
✳ One US size 2 (2.75mm) circular knitting needle
✳ Cable needle

gauge

32 sts and 34 rows to 4in (10cm) square over St st using US size 3 (3.25mm) needles.

abbreviations

M1p make one (M1) purlwise.
C4F slip next 2 sts onto cable needle and hold at front of work, k2, then k2 from cable needle.
Also see page 13.

back

With US size 2 (2.75mm) needles and B, cast on 58(66:74:82:90) sts.

1st row (right side) K2, [p2, k2] to end.

2nd row P2, [k2, p2] to end.

These 2 rows **form** the rib and are repeated.

Change to A.

Work 4 rows more in rib.

Change to B.

Work 2 rows more.

Change and cont in A only.

Work 1 row.

Inc row (wrong side) P2, k2(0:2:0:2), p2(0:2:0:2), [k2, M1p, p2, M1p, k2, p2] to last 4(0:4:0:4) sts, k2(0:2:0:2), p2(0:2:0:2). *70(82:90:102:110) sts.*

Change to US size 3 (3.25mm) needles.

Cont in patt as follows:

1st row (right side) K2, p2(0:2:0:2), k2(0:2:0:2), [p2, k4, p2, k2] to last 4(0:4:0:4) sts, k2(0:2:0:2), p2(0:2:0:2).

2nd row P2, k2(0:2:0:2), p2(0:2:0:2), [k2, p4, k2, p2] to last 4(0:4:0:4) sts, p2(0:2:0:2), k2(0:2:0:2).

3rd row K2, p2(0:2:0:2), k2(0:2:0:2), [p2, C4F, p2, k2] to last 4(0:4:0:4) sts, p2(0:2:0:2), k2(0:2:0:2).

4th row Rep 2nd row.

5th row K2, p2(0:2:0:2), k2(0:2:0:2), [p2, k4, p2, k2] to last 4(0:4:0:4) sts, k2(0:2:0:2), p2(0:2:0:2).

6th row Rep 2nd row.

These 6 rows **form** the pattern and are repeated.

Cont in patt until back measures 4¾(5:5½:6¾:7½)in/ 12(13:14:17:19)cm from cast-on edge, ending with a wrong-side row.

Shape armholes

Bind off 3 sts at beg of next 2 rows. *64(76:84:96:104) sts.* **

Dec one st at each end of next row and 3(5:5:9:9) foll right-side rows. *56(64:72:76:84) sts.*

Cont in patt until back measures 8¾(9½:10¼:11:12)in/ 22(24:26:28:30)cm from cast-on edge, ending with a wrong-side row.

Shape shoulders

Bind off 8(9:10:10:11) sts at beg of next 2 rows and 9(10:11:11:12) sts at beg of foll 2 rows.

Leave rem 22(26:30:34:38) sts on a holder.

front

Work as given for Back to **.

Shape front neck

Next row (right side) Work 2 sts tog, patt 27(33:37:43:47) sts, work 2 sts tog, turn and work on these 29(35:39:45:49) sts only for first side of front neck, leave rem 33(39:43:49:53) sts on a spare needle.

Next row Patt to end.

Next row Work 2 sts tog, patt to last 2 sts, k2tog.

Rep last 2 rows 2(4:4:8:8) times. *23(25:29:27:31) sts rem.*

Keeping armhole edge straight, dec one st at neck edge only on every foll right-side row until 17(19:21:21:23) sts rem.

Work even until front measures same as Back to shoulder, ending at armhole edge.

Shape shoulder

Bind off 8(9:10:10:11) sts at beg of next row.

Work 1 row.

Bind off rem 9(10:11:11:12) sts.

With right side facing, rejoin yarn to sts on spare needle, bind off 1 st, skp, bind off 1 st, patt to last 2 sts, work 2 sts tog.

Next row Patt to end.

Next row Skp, patt to last 2 sts, work 2 sts tog.

Rep the last 2 rows 2(4:4:8:8) times. *23(25:29:27:31) sts rem.*

Keeping armhole edge straight, dec one st at neck edge on every foll right-side row until 17(19:21:22:23) sts rem.

Work even until front measures same as Back to shoulder, ending at armhole edge.

Shape shoulder

Bind off 8(9:10:10:11) sts at beg of next row.

Work 1 row.

Bind off rem 9(10:11:11:12) sts.

collar

Sew shoulder seams.

With right side facing, US size 2 (2.75mm) circular needle and A, pick up and k 36(38:40:44:46) sts evenly up right side of front neck, work p0(0:0:0:2), [k2tog], 0(0:0:2:2) times, k0(0:2:0:0), p0(2:2:2:2), k2, p2, [k2tog] twice, p2, k2, p2, [k2 tog] twice, p2, k2, p0(2:2:2:2), k0(0:2:0:0), [k2tog], 0(0:0:2:2) times, p0(0:0:0:2) across back neck sts, pick up and k 36(38:40:44:46) sts evenly down left side of front neck. *90(98:106:114:122) sts.*

Work in rows not rounds.

1st, 3rd, and 4th sizes only

1st row P2, [k2, p2] to end.

2nd and 5th sizes only

1st row K2, [p2, k2] to end.

All sizes

This row **sets** the rib patt.

Next 2 rows Rib to last 36(36:36:40:40) sts, turn.

Next 2 rows Rib to last 32(32:32:36:36) sts, turn.

Next 2 rows Rib to last 28(28:28:32:32) sts, turn.

Next 2 rows Rib to last 24(24:24:28:28) sts, turn.

Next 2 rows Rib to last 20(20:20:24:24) sts, turn.

4th and 5th sizes only

Next 2 rows Rib to last -(-:-:20:20) sts, turn.

All sizes

Next 2 rows Rib to last 16 sts, turn.

Change to B.

Next 2 rows Rib to last 12 sts, turn.
Change to A.
Next 2 rows Rib to last 8 sts, turn.
Next 2 rows Rib to last 4 sts, turn.
Rib to end.
Change to B.
Next row Rib to end.
With B, bind off in rib.

armbands

With right side facing, US size 2 (2.75mm) needles and A, pick up and
k 78(82:86:94:98) sts evenly around armhole edge.
Change to B.
1st row K2, [p2, k2] to end.
2nd row P2, [k2, p2] to end.
These 2 rows **form** the rib pattern and are repeated.
Rib 4 rows A, and 1 row B.
With B, bind off in rib.

to finish

Lap left front collar over right and sew row ends to bound-off sts at center front.
Sew side and armband seams.

For Home

Teapot Cozy Wrap

There is nothing more comforting that a home-brewed pot of tea. But for me, tea has to be served piping hot, and the only way to ensure this is with a teapot cozy. This cabled aran cover neatly buttons around the teapot so it can be adjusted to fit most sizes; you could even adjust the proportions to suit a cafetiere if the your gift is for a coffee lover rather than a tea drinker.

size
To fit a six-cup teapot

materials
* 1 x 1¾oz (50g) ball of Debbie Bliss Cashmerino Aran in stone
* Pair each of US size 6 (4mm) and US size 7 (4.5mm) knitting needles
* 2 small buttons

gauge
20 sts and 27 rows to 4in (10cm) square over St st using US size 7 (4.5mm) needles.

abbreviations
C4B slip next 2 sts onto cable needle and hold at back of work, k2, then k2 from cable needle.
C4BP slip next 2 sts onto cable needle and hold at back of work, k2, then p2 from cable needle.
C4F slip next 2 sts onto cable needle and hold to front of work, k2, then k2 from cable needle.
C4FP slip next 2 sts onto cable needle and hold to front of work, p2, then k2 from cable needle.
Also see page 13.

pattern A (worked over 14 sts)
1st row (wrong side) K4, p6, k4.
2nd row P4, C4B, C4FP, p2.
3rd row K2, p2, k2, p4, k4.
4th row P4, k4, p2, C4FP.
5th row P2, k4, p4, k4.
6th row P4, C4B, p4, k2.
7th row Rep 6th row.
8th row P4, k4, p2, C4BP.
9th row Rep 4th row.
10th row P4, C4B, C4BP, p2.
11th row Rep 2nd row.
12th row P2, C4BP, C4F, p4.
13th row K4, p4, k2, p2, k2.
14th row C4BP, p2, k4, p4.
15th row K4, p4, k4, p2.
16th row K2, p4, C4F,
17th row Rep 16th row.
18th row C4FP, p2, k4, p4.
19th row K4, p4, k2, p2, k2.
20th row P2, C4FP, C4F, p4.
These 20 rows **form** patt panel A.

pattern B (worked over 14 sts)
1st–10th rows Rep 11th–20th rows of Patt A.
11th–20th rows Rep 1st–10th rows of Patt A.
These 20 rows **form** patt panel B.

to make
With US size 6 (4mm) needles, cast on 102 sts.
1st row (right side) K2, [p2, k2] to end.
2nd row K2, p to last 2 sts, k2.
3rd (buttonhole) row K2, p2tog, yo, k2, [p2, k2] to end.
4th row K2, p to last 2 sts, k2.
Rep 1st and 2nd rows once more.
Change to US size 7 (4.5mm) needles.
Next row (right side) K2, p6, [k6, p8] twice, k6, p7, k2, turn and cont on these 51 sts only, leave rem 51 sts on a holder.
1st row (wrong side) K5, [work across 14 sts of 1st row of Patt A] 3 times, k4.

2nd row K2, p2, [work across 14 sts of 2nd row of Patt A] 3 times, p3, k2.
These 2 rows **set** the position of 3 patt panels with reverse St st and 2 sts in garter st at each end and are repeated 9 times more, working correct patt panel rows. When all 20 patt panel rows have been worked, rep 1st row once more.
Change to US size 6 (4mm) needles.
Dec row (right side) K2, [p2, k2] 3 times, [p2tog, p1, k2, p1, p2tog, k2, p2, k2] twice, p2tog, p1, k2, p1, p2tog, k1. *45 sts.*
Leave these 45 sts on a holder.
With right side facing and 4.5mm (US 7) needles, rejoin yarn to 51 sts on first holder, k2, p7, [k6, p8] twice, k6, p6, k2.
1st row (wrong side) K4, [work across 14 sts of 1st row of Patt B] 3 times, k5.
2nd row K2, p3, [work across 14 sts of 2nd row of Patt B] 3 times, p2, k2.
These 2 rows **set** the position of 3 patt panels with reverse St st and 2 sts in garter st at each end and are repeated 9 times more, working correct patt panel rows. When all 20 patt panel rows have been worked, rep 1st row once more.
Change to US size 6 (4mm) needles.
Dec row (right side) K1, p2tog, p1, k2, p1, p2tog, [k2, p2, k2, p2tog, p1, k2, p1, p2tog] twice, [k2, p2] 3 times, k2. *45 sts.*
Joining row (wrong side) K4, [p2, k2] to last 6 sts, p2, k4. *90 sts.*
Next row K2, [p2, k2] to end.
Next row K4, [p2, k2] to last 6 sts, p2, k4.
Rep the last 2 rows 3 times more.
Dec row (right side) K2, [k2tog] to last 2 sts, k2. *47 sts.*
Next row K2, p to last 2 sts, k2.
Buttonhole row K1, k2tog, k to end.
Next row K2, p to last 2 sts, k2.
Next row K to end.
Rep the last 2 rows once more. Bind off knitwise.

to finish
Sew on buttons. Wrap around teapot and fasten buttons above and below handle.

Hot-Water Bottle Cover

When the weather has cooled and it's chilly both inside and out, a warming hot-water bottle is the ultimate comfort. Wrapped in a soft knitted cover, the plainest hot-water bottle is transformed into a thoughtful present. The simplicity of the textured ridge stitch is enhanced by this pastel pink, but you could plump for a neutral color or even a brighter shade to complement an interior.

size
To fit a standard hot-water bottle from base to top of neck—8¼in x 13in (21cm x 33cm)

materials
✳ Two 1¾oz (50g) balls of Debbie Bliss Cashmerino Aran in pale pink
✳ Pair of US size 7 (4.5mm) knitting needles

gauge
19 sts and 36 rows to 4in (10cm) square over patt using US size 7 (4.5mm) needles.

abbreviations
See page 13.

pattern
1st row (right side) K to end.
2nd row K to end.
3rd row K to end.
4th row P to end.
5th row P to end.
6th row P to end.
These 6 rows **form** the pattern and are repeated throughout.

to make
Worked in one piece from the base.
With US size 7 (4.5mm) needles, cast on 75 sts.
Work in patt, as given above, until piece measures 9in (23cm) from cast-on edge or until it reaches the start of the shoulder of your bottle, ending with a 2nd patt row.
Shape shoulders
1st row (right side) K17, skp, k2tog, k33, skp, k2tog, k17.
2nd row P16, p2tog tbl, p2tog, k31, p2tog tbl, p2tog, p16.
3rd row P15, p2tog tbl, p2tog, k29, p2tog tbl, p2tog, p15.
4th row P14, p2tog tbl, p2tog, k27, p2tog tbl, p2tog, p14.

5th row K13, skp, k2tog, k25, skp, k2tog, k13.
6th row K to end.
7th row K12, skp, k2tog, k23, skp, k2tog, k12.
8th row P to end.
9th row P11, p2tog tbl, p2tog, k21, p2tog tbl, p2tog, p11.
10th row P to end.
11th row K10, skp, k2tog, k19, skp, k2tog, k10.
12th row K to end.
13th row K9, skp, k2tog, k17, skp, k2tog, k9.
14th row P to end.
15th row P8, p2tog tbl, p2tog, k15, p2tog tbl, p2tog, p8.
35 sts.
Work even in patt for 15 rows more, so ending with a 2nd patt row.
Bind off purlwise on right side, loosely but evenly.

to finish
Sew together the row ends to form the center back seam, matching the ridge rows.
Sew the base seam.
Insert the hot-water bottle into the finished cover before filling.

Seed Stitch Table Mats

Knitted in practical seed stitch in a robust washable cotton yarn, these mats offer a simple way to add color to any table setting. When it comes to the color pairings, literally anything goes. Make an entire set of these mats for all the members of your family, with a different color combination for each person so everybody knows their place at the table.

size
Approximately 10¼in x 8in (26cm x 21cm)

materials
4 mats
✻ 2 x 1¾oz (50g) balls of Debbie Bliss Cotton DK in each of chocolate, stone, lime, pale green, teal, duck egg blue, fuchsia, and red (see Note)
✻ Pair of US size 10½ (7mm) knitting needles

gauge
12 sts and 20 rows to 4in (10cm) square over seed st using US size 10½ (7mm) needles and the yarn double.

abbreviations
See page 13.

note
Each mat is double sided and worked with 2 strands of yarn. You will need 2 balls of yarn for each side of each mat.

to make
Work one mat in each shade.
With US size 10½ (7mm) needles and using the yarn double, cast on 25 sts.
Seed st row K1, [p1, k1] to end.
Rep this row until work measures 10¼in (26cm).
Bind off.

to finish
Pair up fuchsia with chocolate, stone with red, teal with pale green, and lime with duck egg blue, and sew together the pairs around the four sides.

Pot of Pansies

These knitted pansies are the ultimate hardy perennials. If you want to give a floral gift, but you know the recipient doesn't have a green thumb, these woolen flowers are the perfect choice. With no need to water, they provide an everlasting splash of cheery color all year round.

size
Knitted cover to fit a 4¼in (11cm) flower pot

materials
* 1 x 1¾oz (50g) ball of Debbie Bliss Rialto DK in rust, purple, green, and gold and 1 x 1¾oz (50g) ball of Debbie Bliss Riva in brown
* Pair each of US size 6 (4mm), US size 8 (5mm), and US size 10½ (7mm) knitting needles
* Set of four US size 6 (4mm) double-pointed knitting needles
* 4¼in (11cm) terracotta flower pot
* Floral foam to fit pot or cut down to fit
* Florists wire
* Green plastic-coated wire
* Copydex glue or similar waterbased adhesive

gauge
22 sts and 30 rows 4in (10cm) square over St st using US size 6 (4mm) needles and Rialto DK for flower pot cover.

abbreviations
sk2p slip one knitwise, k2tog, pass slipped st over.
Also see page 13.

flowerpot

With US size 6 (4mm) needles and rust, cast on 43 sts.
Beg with a k row, work 21 rows in St st, increasing 1 st
at each end of 5th row and 4 foll 4th rows. *51 sts.*
Ridge row (wrong side) [With left-hand needle, pick up
loop of corresponding st 4 rows below and with right-
hand needle, p this st and next st on left-hand needle
tog] to end.
Change to US size 8 (5mm) needles and beg with a k
row, work 15 rows in St st.
Cut yarn and thread through sts on needle, do not pull up.
Sew the seam.

leaves

** With US size 6 (4mm) double-pointed needles and
green, cast on 3 sts and make a cord as follows:
1st row K3.
Next row Slide the sts to the opposite end of the needle
without turning, pull the yarn tightly across the wrong
side from left to right and k one row. **
Rep the last 2 rows until cord measures ¾in (2cm).
Now cont in rows as follows:
1st row (right side) K1, [yo, k1] twice. *5 sts.*
2nd row K2, p1, k2.
3rd row K2, yo, k1, yo, k2. *7 sts.*

4th row K3, p1, k3.
5th row K3, yo, k1, yo, k3. *9 sts.*
6th row K4, p1, k4.
7th row K4, yo, k1, yo, k4. *11 sts.*
8th row K5, p1, k5.
9th row K5, yo, k1, yo, k5. *13 sts.*
10th row K to end.
11th row Ssk, k to last 2 sts, k2tog.
Rep the last 2 rows 3 times more. *5 sts.*
18th row K to end.
19th row Ssk, k1, k2tog. *3 sts.*
20th row K to end.
21st row Sk2p and fasten off.

large petals (make 4)

With US size 6 (4mm) needles and purple, cast on 8 sts.
Beg with a k row, work 4 rows in St st.
Cont in St st and inc 1 st at each end of next row and foll
k row. *12 sts.*
P 1 row.
Cont in St st and dec 1 st at each end of next row and
foll k row. *8 sts.*
P 1 row.
Bind off.

smaller petals (make 6)

With US size 6 (4mm) needles and gold, cast on 8 sts.
Beg with a k row, work 4 rows in St st.
Cont in St st and inc 1 st at each end of next row. *10 sts.*
P 1 row.
Cont in St st and dec 1 st at each end of next row. *8 sts.*
P 1 row.
Bind off.

pansy stems (make 2)

With US size 6 (4mm) needles and green, cast on 6 sts.
Beg with a k row, work 2in (5cm) in St st.
Bind off.

bud

With US size 6 (4mm) needles and purple, cast on 4 sts.
Beg with a k row, work 10 rows in St st.
Change to gold and work 6 rows.
Bind off.
Roll the strip with the gold in the middle and sew the
cast-on edge down to form a tight tube.

bud leaf

Work as Leaves from ** to **.
Rep the last 2 rows until cord measures 2in (5cm).
Cont in rows as follows:
Next row K1, [yo, k1] twice. *5 sts.*
P 1 row.
Next row K1, [yo, k1] 4 times. *9 sts.*
P 1 row.
Next row K1, [yo, k1] 8 times. *17 sts.*
Next row Bind off 1 st, [slip st back onto left needle, cast
on 2 sts, bind off 5 sts] to end.
Fasten off.

soil

With US size 10½ (7mm) needles and brown and cast on
5 sts.
Next row K1, [p1, k1] to end.
This row **forms** the seed st and is repeated.
Working inc sts into seed st, inc one st at each end of
next row and 5 foll alt rows. *17 sts.*
Work 2 rows in seed st.
Dec one st at each end of next row and 5 foll alt rows.
5 sts.
Work 1 row in seed st.
Bind off.

to finish

petals

With right side facing and starting from center of each bound-off edge, thread florists wire around the outer edge of each petal, stretching the knitting slightly and leaving 2¼in (6cm) of wire free at each end. Overcast stitch the edge with matching yarn. Twist the two ends of wire together.

leaves

Thread green plastic-coated wire up through the stem, around the leaf and back down through the stem, leaving 3¼in (8cm) of wire free at each end. Twist the two ends of wire together.

bud

Wrap the bud leaf around the bud and secure. Thread green plastic-coated wire through stem and into the base of the bud and leaf, leaving about 3¼in (8cm) of wire free.

pansies

For the stem, cut a 4in (10cm) length of green plastic-coated wire, then arranging the petals as in picture to form a pansy "face" with two large purple petals behind three gold petals, twist the petal wire around the stem wire. For each flower, wrap the pansy stem around the wires and sew together the row ends, leaving about 3¼in (8cm) of wire free and sew stem to base of pansy, with seam at back. Using purple yarn, embroider a few long stitches onto the gold petals.

pot

Push the floral foam into the pot, cutting to size if necessary and leaving about 1¼in (3cm) space at the top. Place the pot cover over the pot, folding the excess over the top edge and gluing in place, also glue around the bottom edge of the pot to hold the cast-on edge of the cover in place. Place the knitted soil on the top of the floral foam, thread the stems of the leaves, the pansies and bud through the soil and push into the floral foam as far as possible to hold in place, arranging them as in the photograph or as preferred.

"Home Is Where the Heart Is" Pillow

This heart and home motif pillow makes the perfect housewarming gift to celebrate moving-in day. Worked in intarsia on stockinette stitch, you could easily adjust the house shape to mirror the silhouette of the recipient's home. Or you could simply knit up the pillow incorporating just the heart motif as a special present for a loved one on Valentine's Day.

size
Approximately 16in x 16in (41cm x 41cm)

materials
✳ 4 x 1¾oz (50g) balls of Debbie Bliss Cashmerino Aran in ruby (A) and 1 x 1¾oz (50g) ball in ecru (B)
✳ Pair of US size 8 (5mm) knitting needles
✳ 16in (41cm) square pillow form
✳ 3 buttons

gauge
18 sts and 24 rows to 4in (10cm) square over St st using US size 8 (5mm) needles.

abbreviations
yo2 yarn over right needle twice to make 2 stitches.
Also see page 13.

to make

With US size 8 (5mm) needles and A, cast on 77 sts.

Seed st row K1, [p1, k1] to end.

Rep this row 3 times more.

Beg with a k row, work 15 rows in St st, so ending with a k row.

Ridge row (wrong side) K to end.

Beg with a k row, cont in St st for 20 rows more.

Next row K23, k across 31 sts of 1st row of chart, k23.

Next row P23, p across 31 sts of 2nd row of chart, p23.

These 2 rows **set** the position of the chart and are repeated.

Cont until all 61 rows have been worked.

Beg with a p row, cont in St st in A only for 20 rows more, so ending with a k row.

Ridge row (wrong side) K to end.

Beg with a k row, work 88 rows in St st, so ending with a p row.

Buttonhole row [K16, skp, yo2, k2tog] 3 times, k17.

Next row P to end, working [p1, p1 tbl] into each yo2.

Work 4 rows in seed st.

Bind off in seed st.

to finish

Fold cover along ridge rows and sew side seams from fold to cast-on edge, then sew side seams from fold to bound-off edge, working through all thicknesses where cover overlaps. Sew on buttons. Insert pillow form and fasten buttons.

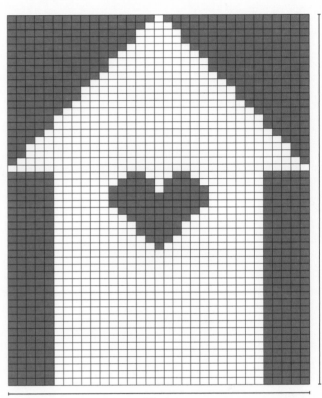

52 rows

33 sts

Key

■ A

☐ B

Striped Pencil Holder Cover

I love the colorful organization that these holders bring to my work desk at home. However, these super-simple striped covers needn't be just for pencils. The pattern can easily be adjusted to suit any size container, so you can tailor them to fit any vessel; why not team the stripes with a friend's favorite color to make a cover for a flower vase or even a tall jar to house knitting needles.

size

To fit a 4in (10cm) tall straight-sided container (see end of instructions for other sizes)

materials

* Small amount of Debbie Bliss Rialto DK in each of four colors (A, B, C, and D—see Note).
* Pair of US size 5 (3.75mm) knitting needles

gauge

24 sts and 42 rows to 4in (10cm) square over garter st using US size 5 (3.75mm) needles.

note

Approximately 8g in each of navy (A), lime (B), burnt orange (C), and teal (D) was used for the covers pictured.

abbreviations

See page 13.

to make

With US size 5 (3.75mm) needles and D, cast on 24 sts using the two-needle knit-on cable cast-on method.

1st row (wrong side) K to end.
Working in garter st (k every row), cont in 2 row stripes of A, B, C, and D until the strip, when very slightly stretched, fits around the container, ending, where possible, with a two row stripe in A.
Bind off in D.
Sew the cast-on and bound-off edges together.

to resize the cover

Measure the height of your container, then using the gauge of 24 sts to 4in (10cm)— 6 sts to 1in or 2.4 sts to 1cm—calculate the number of sts you will need to cast on. For example: if you are using a container which is 5in tall, multiply 5 x 6 = 30 sts, so you would cast on 30 sts.

For suppliers of Debbie Bliss yarns please contact:

USA
Knitting Fever Inc.
315 Bayview Avenue
Amityville
NY 11701
USA
t: +1 (516) 546 3600
w: www.knittingfever.com

CANADA
Diamond Yarns Ltd.
155 Martin Ross Avenue
Unit 3
Toronto
Ontario M3J 2L9
Canada
t: +1 (416) 736 6111
w: www.diamondyarn.com

UK & WORLDWIDE DISTRIBUTORS
Designer Yarns Ltd
Units 8–10
Newbridge Industrial Estate
Pitt Street
Keighley
West Yorkshire BD21 4PQ
UK
t: +44 (0) 1535 664222
e: enquiries@designeryarns.uk.com
w: www.designeryarns.uk.com

MEXICO
Estambres Crochet SA de CV
Aaron Saenz 1891-7
Col. Santa Maria
Monterrey
N.L. 64650
Mexico
t: +52 (81) 8335 3870
e: abremer@redmundial.com.mx

DENMARK
Fancy Knit
Hovedvejen 71, 8586 Oerum Djurs
Ramten
Denmark
t: +45 59 46 21 89
e: roenneburg@mail.dk

FINLAND
Eiran Tukku
Mäkelänkatu 54 B
00510 Helsinki
Finland
t: +358 50 346 0575
e: maria.hellbom@eirantukku.fi
w: www.eirantukku.fi

FRANCE
Plassard Diffusion
La Filature
71800 Varennes-sous-Dun
France
t: +33 (0) 3 8528 2828
e: info@laines-plassard.com

GERMANY/AUSTRIA/ SWITZERLAND/ BENELUX
Designer Yarns (Deutschland) GmbH
Welserstraße 10g
D-51149 Köln
Germany
t: +49 (0) 2203 1021910
e: info@designeryarns.de
w: www.designeryarns.de

ICELAND
Storkurinn ehf
Laugavegi 59
101 Reykjavík
Iceland
t: +354 551 8258
e: storkurinn@simnet.is

SPAIN
Oyambre Needlework SL
Balmes, 200 At. 4
08006 Barcelona
Spain
t: +34 (0) 93 487 26 72
e: info@oyambreonline.com

SWEDEN
Nysta garn och textil
Hogasvagen 20
S-131 47 Nacka
Sweden
t: +46 708 81 39 54
e: info@nysta.se
w: www.nysta.se

RUSSIA
Golden Fleece Ltd
Soloviyny proezd 16
117593 Moscow
Russia
t: +8 (903) 000 1967
e: natalya@rukodelie.ru
w: www.rukodelie.ru

NORWAY
Viking of Norway
Bygdaveien 63
4333 Oltedal
Norway
e: post@viking-garn.no
w: www.viking-garn.no

CHINA
Lotus Textile Co Ltd.
77 Zhonghua W. St.
Xingtai
Hebei, 05-4000
China
e: hanpsheng@yahoo.com.cn

AUSTRALIA/NEW ZEALAND

Prestige Yarns Pty Ltd.
P.O. Box 39, Bulli
NSW 2516
Australia
t: +61 (0) 2 4285 6669
e: info@prestigeyarns.com
w: www.prestigeyarns.com

HONG KONG

East Unity Company Ltd
Unit B2
7/F Block B
Kailey Industrial Centre
12 Fung Yip Street
Chan Wan
t: (852) 2869 7110
e: eastunity@yahoo.com.hk

TAIWAN

U-Knit
1F, 199-1 Sec
Zhong Xiao East Road
Taipei
Taiwan
t: +886 2 27527557
e: shuindigo@hotmail.com

THAILAND

Needle World Co Ltd
Pradit Manoontham Road
Bangkok 10310
Thailand
t: +662 933 9167
e: needle-world.coltd@googlemail.com

BRAZIL

Quatro Estacoes Com
Las Linhas e Acessorios Ltda
Av. Das Nacoes Unidas
12551-9 Andar
Cep 04578-000 Sao Paulo
Brazil
t: +55 11 3443 7736
e: cristina@4estacoeslas.com.br

For more information on my other
books and yarns, please visit
www.debbieblissonline.com